LAVENDER

Pamela Allardice

Illustrated by Simone Bennett

Hill of Content

Special Note

All plants, like all medicines, may be dangerous if used improperly. The simple, traditional remedies in this book must not be used as substitutes for professional medical attention to any serious health disturbance. When in doubt, consult your doctor.

First published in Australia 1990
by Hill of Content Publishing
86 Bourke Street, Melbourne
Reprinted 1991, 1993

© Copyright Text: Pamela Allardice
© Illustrations: Simone Bennett

Designed by Sharon Carr
Typeset by Midland Typesetters, Maryborough, Victoria
Printed and bound in Singapore
by Kyodo Printing Pte Ltd

National Library of Australia
Cataloguing-in-Publication data

Allardice, Pamela, Date–
    Lavender.
    ISBN 0 85572 197 9.
    1. Lavenders. I. Title.
635.93387

Confusion has arisen over nomenclature of the lavenders, notably the variety known as 'English lavender', and this book does not purport to resolve any horticultural debate.

To assist readers who wish to identify and grow a lavender plant for their own enjoyment, all the different names it could be known by have been listed in the section 'Varieties'.

Every attempt has been made to verify these names but the author recognises that differences of opinion will continue to exist.

FOR AMANDA

whose friendship is as refreshing as the scent of lavender

Contents

Lavender Lore

Not only is lavender a beautiful and useful plant—it is also surrounded by a host of legends and fairy tales.

Sometimes referred to as 'Our Lady's Candlestick', lavender was a holy plant. Its scent could indeed be a heavenly one, for when the gentle Virgin Mary spread the Infant Jesus' clothes on a bush to dry, she is said to have bestowed on lavender its soft perfume in gratitude.

An old saying runs—"As Rosemary is to the Spirit, so Lavender is to the Soul". Perhaps it is derived from the belief that these two plants faithfully accompanied Adam and Eve when they were expelled from Paradise, and God blessed the humble herbs and bid them use their health-giving powers and refreshing fragrance to ease Man's earthly travail.

Thus was born the official view that the Devil, as the harbinger of disease and ill fortune, was repelled by lavender. A very old parable tells of a dairymaid, about to be seduced by the Devil in the guise of a young nobleman, who was saved from a fate worse than death when her suitor took fright because she proffered a posy as a troth token.

A popular anti-witch talisman were lavender flowers bound into the shape of a cross and hung over the door,

The most famous of the nose-herbs is this Lavender, whose flower spike, as modest in hue as a Quaker's bonnet, is highly fragrant.

The Fragrant Garden, by L.B. Wilder

and a garter of green lavender was worn by Irish brides as protection against sorcery. Sprigs were laid with Church vestments, causing Thomas Hood to write of "... the Solemn Clerk who goes lavender'd and shorn".

Old superstitions die hard. Even today, in Tuscany, children carry lavender in their pockets to protect them from being kidnapped by gipsies, and girls of the Karbyll tribe wear flowers to avert their husband's ill temper.

It is therefore suprising that lavender came to symbolise distrust or caution in the classical language of flowers. It was even said that the asp which poisoned Cleopatra habitually lurked beneath a lavender bush, and country folk will still advise you to approach a clump with caution.

In ancient times, lavender was cultivated in the fabled lost continent of Lemuria, believed to be the home of the Garden of Eden. This ancient civilisation produced many fine botanists, who passed on their knowledge of herbs and flowers to the physicians of Atlantis and, in turn, to Egypt.

The Egyptians grew lavender, or 'Indian Spike', in the sacred walled garden of Thebes, and dried the flowers by burying them in terracotta crocks. Lavender's perfume accompanied every Egyptian through his life and remained with him in his tomb, being one of the unguents used by priests in their elaborate rituals of mummification. When the perfume urns in Tutankhamen's burial chamber were opened in 1922, the scent sealed in 3000 years before "to scent the desert and the dead" was—lavender.

Through Asia and Europe, the lavender plant became known as 'nard', nardus' or sometimes 'spikenard'. Dr Fernie, in his 17th century manuscript *Herbal Simples*, refers to it thus:

It is the wonder and joy of the south in its blue dress, and its scent is God's gift to earth.

Maurice Messegue

"By the Greeks, the name Nardus is given to Lavender from Nardus, a city of Syria near the Euphrates, and many persons call the plant 'Nard'. St. Mark mentions this as Spikenard, a thing of great value ... in Pliny's time, blossoms of the Nardus sold for a hundred Roman denarii the pound ..."

Along with many other perfumes, lavender had a great religious and social significance in the early world. Whereas nowadays summit meetings are held about oil, in those days they were held about perfume; and, because lavender was quite a costly fragrance, it held strong bargaining power. For instance, when the Queen of Sheba determined to secure a trade contract with King Solomon, she flattered him with outrageously extravagant gifts—"myrrh, frankincense, spike, gold, jewels . . ." and, finally, herself.

Another exotic and desirable heroine, who made good use of lavender, was Judith. She saved her native city by seducing and then murdering the Assyrian commander, Holofernes. Her preparatory toilette saw her dry herself with swans' feathers after washing, and then anoint her breasts and arms with the finest imported oils, including ". . . cedar, myrrh, cypress and spike". The result? "The Lord . . . gave her more beauty, so she appeared to all men's eyes incomparably lovely".

The Greek philosopher, Apollonius, noted that whilst "the iris is best at Elis, the perfume made from roses is most excellent at Pharselis . . . the essence of Nard is best at Tarsus". These early Greeks did little for lavender's reputation, using the flowers to deck their virgin victims before sacrificing them to savage gods. However, the hetarii, or courtesans, popularised its scent. They perfumed their breath by holding lavender oil in their mouths and rolling it around with their tongues, and took lavender sitz baths to protect themselves from infection.

Nor was it an inexpensive cosmetic. Martial in his Epigrams complained that his pretty young mistress had demanded from him ". . . a pound of Nard, or a like-priced pair of sardonyxes". He was further heard to grumble "whether the girl is worthy of these things, I do wish".

Roman women used an aromatic compound named 'nardinum', which contained lilies, lavender and myrrh. They also rubbed lavender oil into their scalps to deter lice and filled special brackets carved in their bedposts with the flowers to keep the bed bugs at bay. It was the Romans who began the association of lavender with freshness that has lasted to this day—the very name 'lavender' is derived from the middle Latin *lavare*, meaning 'to wash'.

Here's flowers for you: hot lavender, mints, savory, marjoram . . . the marigold that goes to bed wi' the sun and with him rises, weeping . . .

The Winter's Tale, by W Shakespeare, 1608

The first invention of a perfume was that of lavender water. This has been traditionally credited to the Benedictine Abbess Hildegard, who grew lavender in her garden at Bingen-on-the-Rhine during the 12th century. Her recipe was highly prized in Chaucer's England, where it was a royal favourite:

> "Envie is to the court alway
> For she ne parteth neither night no daie".

Lavender water was then introduced to France by Charlemagne, who planted bushes in his castle gardens to ensure a plentiful supply of the flowers for distillation. Later, the crazed Charles VI—convinced he was made of glass, he demanded courtiers pass comment on the workings of his digestion—ordered white wicker baskets of lavender be hung in the palace to sweeten the air. A keen horseman, he went so far as to have saddlebags of lavender strapped to his horse's belly lest his regal nostrils be affronted by the beast's sweat.

A perfume distilled from lavender and rosemary, known as Hungary Water, began to appear as part of the cosmetic armoury of European ladies in the 14th century. Legend has it that a crippled hermit divulged the secret of its preparation to Queen Elizabeth of Hungary, and assured her it would preserve her youth and beauty for ever. She became so desirable through its use that men were still besotted with her when she was seventy. In fact, when she was seventy-two, the twenty-eight year old King of Poland swore he would die unless he won her hand in marriage.

Subject to migraines, Elizabeth I was known to quaff up to ten cups of lavender tea per day to soothe her troubled brow. However, it was the Virgin Queen's vanity which resulted in the cultivation of great lavender farms, for this was the perfume she favoured above all. She spent extravagantly on fragrance, paying £40 to her 'stillers of swete waters'—enough to provide for them for life—for a single compound. This contained lavender and gillyflower water and promised ". . . to cleanse and keep bright the skynne and flesh and to preserve it in perfect state".

The 'Cavalier Queen', Henrietta Maria introduced the

Hungary Water

Take to every gallon of Brandy or clean Spirits, one handful of Rosemary, one handful of Lavender. I suppose the handfuls to be about a Foot long apiece; and these Herbs must be cut in Pieces about an Inch long. Put these to infuse in the Spirits and, with them, about one handful of Myrtle, cut as before. When this has stood three Days, distil it, and you will have the finest Hungary-Water that can be.

The Country Housewife and Lady's
Director R Bradley, 1732

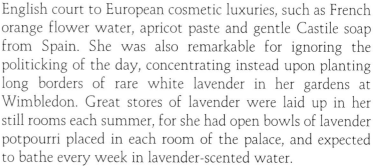

In a black oak chest all carven,
We found it laid,
Still faintly sweet of Lavender
An old Brocade.
With that perfume came a vision,
A garden fair,
Enclosed by great yew hedges;
A lady there,
Is culling fresh blown Lavender,
And singing goes
Up and down the alleys green—
A human rose.

The Old Brocade, by M G Brereton

English court to European cosmetic luxuries, such as French orange flower water, apricot paste and gentle Castile soap from Spain. She was also remarkable for ignoring the politicking of the day, concentrating instead upon planting long borders of rare white lavender in her gardens at Wimbledon. Great stores of lavender were laid up in her still rooms each summer, for she had open bowls of lavender potpourri placed in each room of the palace, and expected to bathe every week in lavender-scented water.

Louis XIV, the Sun King, dearly loved lavender. Called in his own day 'the sweetest-scented monarch the world has ever seen', he even had pages whose job it was to see that his shirts were rinsed in his own special perfume— made by simmering lavender blooms, marjoram and nutmeg in orange water for twenty-four hours.

Madame de Pompadour, mistress of Louis XV, lavished lavender water upon herself, as did Marie Antoinette. The latter re-popularised the pleasure of the fragrant bath, almost forgotten in Europe since the fall of Rome. Her favourite recipe was a sticky mixture of milk, honey, lavender oil and rose petals.

Eau de Cologne was the new scent during the time of the Empress Josephine. Based on citrus oils, bergamot and lavender, it was an immediate success and was named in honour of the Empress—Eau de Cologne Imperiale. This was also Napoleon's favourite perfume and he used it extravagantly throughout his life. Even on campaign he would pour it over his neck and shoulders every time he washed.

Eau de Cologne started the fashion for gentle, lavender-scented toilet waters that has lasted until our own day. By the 19th century, the fondest adherent was the doughty Queen Victoria herself. Said to obtain her lavender ". . . direct from a lady who distills it herself", a contemporary court gossip assures us that "the Royal Residences are thoroughly impregnated with the refreshing perfume of this old-fashioned flower, and there is none that the Queen likes better". A true romantic, Victoria's heart was quite lost when her dear Albert came a-courtin' with nosegays of lavender and heather. She became a fastidious housekeeper on her

Lavender Water

Put two pounds of lavender pipps in two quarts of water; put them into a cold still, and make a slow fire under it; distil off very slowly into a pot till you have distilled all your water; then clean your still well out, put your lavender into it and distil it off slowly again; put it into bottles and cork well.

The New Art of Cookery, by Richard Briggs many years Cook at the Globe Tavern, Fleet Street, the White Hart Tavern, Holborn, and the Temple Coffee House, 1788.

marriage, and insisted that the oaken shelves of her linen presses be polished with lavender oil until they gleamed.

Around this time today's best-known lavender water, Yardley's came into being when William Yardley, a sword-maker, took over his son-in-law's failed soap and perfumery business. Fashionable men were starting to go wigless and, to display their hair to the best advantage, were using a variety of scented pomades. Recognising this, Yardley produced a dressing of bear's grease and lavender oil which became a best seller and spearheaded a wide variety of lavender products. And the famous engraving of a lavender seller crying "Buy my sweet lavender, two bunches a penny!" which is found on Yardley's products? Well, she was once a primrose seller. Yardley's touched out the primroses in Francis Wheatley's original in order to advertise their products.

Royal patronage of this wholesome flower continues. Yardley of London are suppliers by appointment of lavender water, talc and soap to both Queen Elizabeth II and the Queen Mother. It remains a firm favourite amongst the English, having become almost emblematic of that isle where there are

> Gay cottage gardens, glad,
> comely, unkempt and mad,
> Jumbled, jolly and quaint;
> Nooks where some old man dozes;
> Currants and beans and roses
> Mingling without restraint;
> A wicket that long lacks paint;
> Here grows Lavender, here breathes England.
>
> Wilfrid Blair, *Lavender*, 1917

Lavender and Love

With its tender fragrance, long-lasting flowers and soft colour reminiscent of halcyon summer days, lavender inspired Symons to pen *Memory*:-

> "As the perfume doth remain
> In the folds where it hath lain
> So the thought of you, remaining
> Deeply folded in my brain
> Will not leave me: all things leave me
> You remain."

Lavender is certainly assured a place in the romantic lore of flowers. As Scott observed ". . . even the old maid has her little romance carefully preserved in the lavender of memory." That lavender was often a token of remembrance between sweethearting couples is evidenced by these gently contemplative lines from Lady Lindsay:

"Lavender grey, lavender blue
Perfume wrapt in the sky's own hue;
Lavender blue, lavender grey
Love in memory, lives alway;
Lavender grey, lavender blue
Sweet is remembrance if love be true;
Lavender blue, lavender grey
Sweeter methinks, is the love of today."

It also featured in popular rhymes for St Valentine's Day:

"Lilies are white, rosemary's green;
When you are king, I will be queen.
Roses are red, lavender's blue—
If you will have me, then I will have you."

A particularly sentimental verse from a Victorian Valentine card—appropriately printed on lavender-scented parchment decorated with a frilled, lacy heart, runs:-

"A violet breath
That opes with magic key
The inmost chambers of my heart
And sets its sweetest mem'ries free."

Leigh Hunt wrote of "pure lavender, to lay in bridal gown", for the scent would waft from hope chests where young girls had tenderly tucked sachets amongst the nuptial linens and lawns. Polish bridesmaids wore bags of dried lavender and lovage between their breasts in the hope of attracting a sweetheart, and it even became customary to quilt lavender into a bridal head-dress, to avoid any wedding night headache. On a more bawdy note, one of the Elizabethan poets, Robert Green, has a character advise his son that to win his lady-love he should hide in her linen press so that ". . . she may lay thee up in lavender and put thee upon"!

"The sprays of gray-green (which) . . . keep till you're old" have long been a favourite troth-token between lovers. During his secret meetings with Nell Gwynn, Charles II

Those that do use the flowers in sallets to exhilerate and make the mind well. There be also many thynges made of these used . . . for the comfort of the heart, the driving away of sorrow and increasing joy . . .

The Herball, by John Gerard, 1597

was wont to give her 'swete bags' of dried lavender tied up with gold ribbon. Another charming Stuart custom saw lovers exchanging pretty bottles of deliciously scented "swete waters", made from distilled bay leaves, lavender and clove pinks.

A tisane of lavender flowers, ice and honey was imbibed by sweethearts before their assignations for its invigorating effect. Similarly, Napoleon favoured a drink combining equal parts of chocolate, musk and coffee with a dash of lavender sugar, and took a wineglassful before entering Josephine's apartments. Elderly French gentlemen are still dosed with this potion—presumably the high sugar content and refreshing aroma help to bolster sagging energy levels.

Lavender flowers candied in caster sugar were first made popular in France as love-provoking sweetmeats, before taking the English court by storm. Dusted with powdered cherry stones and nutmeg, they became known as 'kissing comfits' and were used as breath sweeteners. In the court of the licentious Louis XIV, lavender buds were dipped in ambergris and sent as a gift to a potential mistress. If she popped one in her mouth in view of the King, it signalled an acceptance of his 'invitation'.

In *The Shepherd's Calender*, 19th century poet John Clare describes a lovers' bower in a cottage garden thus:-

> With marjoram knots, sweet brier and ribbongrass
> And lavender, the choice of every lass
> And sprigs of lad's love, all familiar names . . .

In truth, Mr Clare may have been casting ribald aspersions upon the wanton habits of young folk. You see, a warm infusion of southernwood, or 'Lad's Love' and lavender was then one of the few known methods for relieving itching from infections contracted through careless love-making!

Nearly everyone knows the playful 'Dilly Dilly' song :-

> Lavender blue, dilly dilly
> Lavender green
> When I am king, dilly dilly
> You'll be my queen.

The Green Oyle To Be Made In May Called Oyle of Charity

Take Red Sage Rosemary Spanish Lavender with the broad leafe and bawme Camomile Valerian of each fouer ounces wormwood two ounces gather them in a hott Sunny day and wipe them upon a Cloath but do not wash them then cut them very Small and put them into a Convenient Vessell or a Glass if you have it and put to it a quart of the Purest Oyle you can gett and tye it up very close letting it stand in the Sunn a fortnight or three weeks . . .

The Virtues of this Oyle. It is good to anoint and tent all wounds for it will Search to the bottom it will Dead the proud flesh that growes in a wound it Draws out thorns and Splinters and it is excellent for bruises in any part of the body to anoint the place or to give inwardly to Drink tenn or twelve drops for a man or woman half as much to a Child in a Spoonfull of Possett Drink made with ale or White Wine

Book of Receipts, by Thomas Newington, 1719

How to make a Sourveraigne Water that Master Doctor Stevens, Physitian, a man of great knowledge and cunning did practice and used of long experience and therewith did many cures, and kept it always secret, till of late, a little before his death, a special friend of his did get it in writing of him.

Take a gallon of good Gascoigne wine, then take ginger, camomile, cinnamon, nutmegs, cloves, mace, annis seeds, fennell seeds, carroway seeds, of every of them a dramme, then take sage, minte, red Roses, Tyme, Pellitory of the Wall, wild margerum, Rosemary, wild Tyme, Camomile, and lavender of every one of them a handfull, then beat the spices small, and bruise the hearbes, and put all into the wine and let it stand twelve hours, stirring it divers times; then still it in a Limbeck, and keepe the first pinte of the water, for it is the best, then will come a seconde water, which is not so good as the first.

John Partridge,
The Treasurie of Commodius Conceits and Hidden Secrets, 1586

Some may recall it as a nursery rhyme, others as a catchy dance tune sung by Dinah Shore in Walt Disney's 1948 film *So Dear To My Heart*. What they may not know is that the original song, entitled 'Diddle, Diddle, or The Kind Country Lovers' was printed in England in 1680. The verses therein belie the staid woodcut of a lover and his lass on the cover.

> "I heard one say, diddle diddle
> Since I came within
> That you and I diddle diddle
> Must lie together
>
> Call up your maids, diddle diddle
> Sett them to work
> Some to make hay, diddle diddle
> Some to the Rock
>
> Some to make hay, diddle diddle
> Some to the corn
> Whilst you and I, diddle diddle
> Keep the bed warm
>
> Let the birds sing, diddle diddle
> And the lambs play
> We shall be safe, diddle diddle
> Out of harms' way"

Lavender has also had its moment of glory as a love charm. If a Tudor maid wished to see her true love, all she had to do was brew lavender flowers and wild thyme, and simmer them in virgin honey and wine. She then applied the liquid to her lips on St Luke's Day, whilst murmuring:

> St Luke, St Luke, be kind to me
> In dreams let me my true love see.

In Denmark, many an anxious lover would place a posy of St John's Wort and lavender between north-facing roof beams for the purpose of romantic divination on St Valentine's Day. The usual custom was to tie together one sprig of each for herself and another for her sweetheart—

A Sweet-Scented Bath

Take of Roses, Citron Peel, Sweet Flowers, Orange Flowers, Jessamy, Bays, Rosemary, Lavender, Mint, Pennyroyal, of each a sufficient quantity, boil them together gently and make a Bath to which add Oyl of Spike six drops, musk five grains, Ambergris five grains.

From The Receipt Book of
John Middleton, 1734

should they fall together overnight it indicated an approaching wedding.

Maidens of the French Alps would gather the fragrant lavender flowers and place them under their lovers' pillows, for it was considered a potent aphrodisiac. Being the traditional home of lavender, young folk would prove their sweethearts' affection in a pretty ceremony which was held each year. At the close of summer harvest, men carrying bunches of green wheat ears and women wearing garlands of flax blossom congregated in the town square. There, they heaped high wreaths of fresh lavender. If the flowers remained sweet and blue, the lovers named for that wreath would be united. However, if they withered unduly the couple would certainly part.

Jane Austen's heroines carried lavender in their reticules— so refreshing should one have an attack of the vapours when affronted by a handsome young rake. In fact, this ladylike habit derived from magic practised by country 'herb-wyfes'. To treat a girl recovering from the shock of being jilted, a reed locket containing lavender would be tied around her neck for its calming, soothing effect.

Along with basil, lavender was once regarded as a test for chastity, being thought to wither in the hands of the impure. In fact, the flowers were sometimes called upon to test the faith of lovers. Witness Fair Margaret, who selected lavender to tell her the truth about Faust:-

> . . . the maiden found the mystic flower
> 'Now, gentle flower, I pray thee tell
> If my love loves, and loves me well
> So may the fall of the morning dew
> Keep the sun from fading thy tender blue
> He loves me! 'Yes', a dear voice sighed
> And her lover stands by Margaret's side.

Similarly, a Bohemian girl who secreted a sprig of lavender in her lover's right shoe ere he commenced a journey, ensured his fidelity. Seamen's wives took this cue as well, and fed their menfolk caraway and lavender seed cakes before they left on voyages for exotic climes.

For A Bath

Take of Sage, Lavender Flowers, Roseflowers to each two handfuls, a little salt, boil them in water or lye, and make a bath not too hot in which to bathe the Body in a morning, or two hours before Meat.

From the Receipt Book of John Middleton, 1734

Lavender was a happy charm for a newly wed couple. A spray tucked under the nuptial mattress would create and preserve love, as well as warding off mischievous night elves who tweaked hair and caused arguments. Once a favoured strewing herb, lavender was scattered over banqueting tables and in front of wedding processions. Remember to take a basket of lavender buds to the next wedding you attend, and pelt the newly-weds for sweet-scented luck!

Lavender is one of the essential oils which does put you 'in the mood', being physically relaxing and stimulating at the same time. Turn your bathroom into a 'scentual' boudoir experience and restore romance to your life with any of the following ideas:-

φ To create a warm, invigorating atmosphere, place a drop of lavender oil on a warm light bulb. It will soon fill the room with fragrance.

φ Give your lingerie a libidinous air by adding a little lavender essence to the rinsing water next time you wash. You could also sprinkle some on a cotton ball and tuck it into your slip or camisole.

φ Try a romantic bath *à deux* to excite flagging emotions. Run warm water into the tub and add three drops of lavender oil and two drops of rose. Massage each other's feet, neck and shoulders as you luxuriate in the bath. Then, step out of the tub and pat each other dry with warm soft towels.

Take a Gallon of faire water, one handful of Lavender flowers, a few Cloves and some Orace powder and foure ounces of Benjamin; distill the water in an ordinary leaden still. You may distill a second water by a new infusion of water upon the leaves; a little of this will sweeten a bason of faire water for your table.

Delightes for Ladies, by Sir Hugh Platt, 1594

φ Follow with a loving massage, stroking back and shoulders with fine almond oil scented with lavender and ylang-ylang essence.

φ Don't just stop with the basic massage—other parts of the body respond to lavender's tonic effect, too!

Lavender Foot Care

This foot bath will revive your lover's whole body, not just his toes. Combine lavender flowers, sage, thyme and a little sea salt. Steep in boiling water for half an hour and strain. Then, soak feet in liquid, using a pumice stone to smooth away callouses. Use firm strokes, or it will tickle!

Don't Neglect Ears

Take a few drops of lavender oil between your finger and thumb, and gently pinch all round the ear from the outside to the centre. Then trace lightly round the entire area and rub ear lobe.

Hand Massage

Stroke each hand, gently working lavender oil from the base of each finger to the tip, finishing with a gentle tug. Rub the palm with light, circular strokes, concentrating on the energy zones in the base of the thumb.

Look after your Neck

This is a powerful erogenous zone, and is also most prone to aches and tensions—both great incentives for a provocative massage. Brush lavender oil in upward strokes from the shoulders to the base of the skull, kneading gently to ease taut muscles. Follow with little feathery circles from the centre of the head to the ears and back.

A Scottish Handwater

Put Thyme, Lavender and Rosemary confusedly together, then make a lay of thicke wine Lees in the bottom of a stone pot, upon which make another lay of the said hearbs, and then a lay of Lees, and then so forward: lute the pot well, bury it in the ground for six weeks; distill it. A little thereof put into a bason of common water maketh very sweete washing water.

Ram's Little Dadoen, 1606

Ruminating on a slightly lack-lustre love life?

Try this recipe, which belonged to the famed 18th century French courtesan, Ninon de Lenclos. It is said to have worked so well that her grandson, who had never met her before, became besotted with her beauty. Ninon had a difficult time discouraging her youthful suitor's ardour, even when the true nature of their relationship was uncovered!

Take one handful each of lavender, rosemary, mint and thyme. Tie up in a cheesecloth square and steep in boiling water for 10 minutes, or hold under bath tap, allowing hot water to sluice through bag and release fragrance.

A fitting finale to this luscious bath is a light dusting of delicate bath powder. Add lavender oil and a few drops of vanilla extract to equal parts of rice flour and cornstarch; stir the powders and put into a moisture-proof lidded container. The rich, spicy scent of vanilla is the perfect complement to lavender's clean fragrance.

Lavender Gardens

"God Almighty first planted a garden", wrote Francis Bacon, "and indeed it is the purest of human pleasures. It is the greatest refreshment to the spirits of man, without which buildings and palaces are but gross handiwork."

This lively essayist went on to provide a check-list of flowers to provide *ver perpetuum*, or perpetual spring, in a garden throughout the year. Of these, lavender emerged as one of his favourites, both during ". . . December, January and the latter part of November (when) . . . you must take such things as are green all winter", and also during summer, along with ". . . pinks of all sorts, especially the blush pink; roses of all kinds, except the musk . . . honeysuckles; strawberries; cherry tree in fruit; columbine; the French marigold; bugloss; ribes; figs in fruit; rasps, vine flowers, lavender in flowers; the sweet Satyrian with the white flower . . . Herba Muscaria . . ."

Nearly every garden has a lavender bush. It is not surprising that this beautifully scented small shrub has retained its popularity through the centuries. The gray-green foliage and fragrant flowers provide edging for paths and borders. It is also an ideal hedge plant, making it a favourite in many of the older style 'cottage' gardens.

A bonus is that when lavender comes into bloom it will attract the bees and other nectar-seeking insects, which will pollinate all other flowers. Virgil said beehives should be in beds of ". . . fresh lavender and store of wild thyme with strong savory to flower". Honey from hives situated thus has a sublime flavour—no one who has tasted it could ask for sweeter.

Butterflies also favour lavender above all other scents and colours in the garden. In fact, Americans say it is possible to 'call' clouds of tortoiseshell butterflies by waving a branch of lavender in the air.

Fortunately bees and butterflies are amongst the very few insects that enjoy lavender flowers. Caterpillars generally turn up their noses at the strong-scented foliage, as do rabbits—a good point to note for those living in country areas. One pest which can make a mess of a lavender bush is the Light Brown Apple Moth, but the solution is a simple one. Commercial lavender farmers advise encouraging birds to the garden, for they are very partial to this particular grub.

Varieties

Many plant lovers are only aware of 'English' lavender and 'French' lavender. However, there are at least 50 species of lavender and many hybrid cultivars with quite different flower and leaf characteristics, including pink, white, dwarf and blue forms. They all belong to the *Labiatae*, or mint, family.

The two most common varieties are *Lavandula angustifolia* and *Lavandula dentata*.

Lavandula angustifolia—variously known as English lavender, *L. vera*, *L. officinalis* or 'true' lavender, this is the best known variety. The mysterious physicians of Myddvai, who founded European herb lore, named it Llafant. According to Chaytor, most lavenders we see in nurseries are hybrids of 'true' lavender and *Lavandula latifolia* or *L. spica*, the 'Spike' beloved by 16th century herbalists for its pungent, camphoraceous scent.

This flower is good for Bees, most comfortable for smelling except Roses, and kept dry is as strong after a year as when it was gathered. The water is comfortable.

The Country Housewife's Garden, by William Lawson, 1618

French levender being a herbe of very good smell, and very usual in Languedoc and Provence, doth crave to be diligently tilled in a fat ground and lying open to the sunne . . .

The Countrie Farm, Richard Surflet, 1600

Bees and butterflies enjoying lavender in full bloom

Refreshing lavender tea in your favourite garden spot

L. angustifolia is a small shrub with narrowly pointed, smooth grey leaves and a long spike of deep mauve flowers. The scent is superb and it is the variety most commonly farmed for the production of fragrant oil. It is grown commercially in France and also at the Bridestowe Estate in Tasmania. When choosing a variety for drying, this is probably the best, for it is the most potent.

Lavandula dentata, or French lavender, is also known as Lavande. It generally grows into an attractive, bushy shrub about 1 metre high. It has thick, square stems, which bear compact heads of mauve flowers and silver grey serrated leaves throughout the year.

It is almost always in bloom, its main flush being in winter, and it is recommended as a hedge. This variety is particularly happy when planted by a rocky outcrop or stone wall. French lavender's oil yield is three times that of the English type, although it is of an inferior quality.

Lavandula stoechas is also known as Spanish lavender and Italian lavender. The Italians called this variety Spigo or Nardo, while it was known as Stickadove and Steckado to the old herbalists. Spanish lavender has soft, grey-green leaves covered with velvety hairs and the flowers are a rich, dark purple. It blooms in the spring, when its scent is deliciously strong.

*Rarer varieties of lavender include the pink—L. rosea—*and dwarf forms. Both of these are far slower-growing than the purple or blue varieties. There is also a white-flowering lavender—*L. officinalis alba*—with an unforgettably sweet perfume. John Parkinson preferred this above all other lavenders, and wrote fondly in 1629 that ". . . there is a kind hereof that beareth white flowers and somewhat broader leaves, but is very rare and seene but in a few places . . . because it is more tender and will not last so well . . . (and) endure our cold winters."

L. multifida has the most interesting foliage of all the lavenders. The Latin term means 'much-divided', and refers to the lacy, almost fern-like leaves. The fragrance is similar to that of the herb wormwood and the flowers are a rich violet colour.

Stoechas grows in the Islands of Calatia over against Messalia, called ye Stoechades, from whence also it has its name, is an herb with slender twigges, haveing ye haire like Tyme, but yet longer leaved, and sharp in ye taste and somewhat bitterish . . .

Dioscorides, circa 60 AD

Ladies fair, I bring to you
Lavender with spikes of blue;
Sweeter plant was never found
Growing on an English ground.

Carl Battersby, in
A Bunch of Sweet Lavender, by
Constance Isherwood c. 1900

L. allardii is probably the largest specimen of the lavenders. It has grey leaves and flower spikes which can grow up to a metre in length. The whole bush can spread up to 2.5 metres in just over a year.

There is also an unusual green lavender, known as *L. viridis*. This plant has a pine-like scent, narrow sticky leaves and tiny white flowers. Also striking is the *L. stoechas ssp pedunculata*—quite a large plant, it features bright pink flowers with plum-coloured bracts which flower in spring and summer.

Origin and Cultivation

Nearly all lavenders are native to Southern Europe. In 1930 the noted horticulturalist Henri Correvon said ". . . crossing the lavender slopes is one of the most pleasurable experiences of climbers in the Southern Alps, for the delicious odour of the sweet herb persists on clothing to remind them after returning home of the bright sunny regions they travelled."

Mitcham in Surrey was famous for its lavender for nigh on 500 years. Mrs Leyel waxed lyrically in the 1930s that ". . . at Long Melford and Market Deeping, fields of lavender can be seen growing luxuriantly, the beauty of its scent and the immense purple patches of colour make a great appeal to the sense." In fact, special cries were developed by local lavender sellers.

Who'll buy my Mitcham lavender?
It makes your handkerchief so nice
Come along you young ladies and make no delay
I gathered my lavender fresh from Mitcham today
Will you buy my sweet blooming lavender?
There are sixteen dark blue branches a penny
You buy it once, you buy it twice
It will make your cloaths smell sweet and nice
Who'll buy my sweet blooming lavender?
Sixteen full branches a penny.

Today, however, lavender is cultivated much more widely

These herbs do grow wilde in Spaine, in Languedock in France, and the Island called the Stoechades over against Massili; we have them in our gardens and kept with great diligence from the injurie of our colde clymate.

The Herball, John Gerard, 1597

in other parts of England, notably Norfolk and elsewhere in the world, such as Spain, the Saudi Arabian Gulf and the stony fields of Tasmania and Provence.

If you want to dry your lavender or use it inside the house, it is important to plant it in a position which will favour quality flowering. Firstly, from its distribution, we learn that lavenders can tolerate very dry conditions and prefer a light, chalky soil. The grey leaves indicate this, the greyness being really a mass of tiny white hairs which are there to retain moisture.

Do not overfeed bushes. Rich soil or too much fertiliser will give long, soft growth with a lower concentration of oil and, therefore, less scent. If a lavender bush is to be placed in a rich soil area, working a little lime into the soil will benefit it.

The position should preferably face north or north-east with some protection from harsh winds. The other main requirement for strong growth is to plant out in an open position, where the soil is freely drained. While lavenders can withstand arid conditions and sandy soil, they will not be able to cope if their roots become waterlogged.

Ensure a healthy, well-shaped shrub with regular hard pruning in autumn. This will actually produce flowers over a much longer period. Young plants should be pruned, rather than allowed to flower, in order to encourage strong bushy growth. Always be sure to leave green wood below the trim line and not to clip the old wood. Don't waste the prunings, either. The leaves should be gathered up straight away and put into a large earthenware pot in preparation for making potpourri. Or throw them on the barbeque to add a new flavour to food.

Propagation

Lavenders can be cultivated from seed or propagated by root divisions and cuttings. The latter is the most common method, since seed is not generally available to home gardeners. Spring cuttings are usually taken, although they can also be obtained from young growth in autumn.

Cut a section of new growth about 5 cm long and remove leaves and shoots from base before planting in a propagating mix. A fairly humid atmosphere favours striking, which should occur within 6 weeks if a hormone fertiliser is used, 8 weeks if not. New plants may be bedded into the garden as soon as they have formed a strong root system, but it is best to wait until spring in order to avoid any frost which could harm the delicate tips.

Garden Design

Hawes wrote in 1554 of ". . . an arber, fayre to Paradise, right well comparable, set all about with flowers fragrant." How right he was—however small your garden, endeavour to plant a bower or nook where you may sit and be refreshed by the scent of lavender.

This idea of a little garden within a larger one came from the Romans who designed enchanting toy gardens, featuring lavender bushes and box trees clipped in formal and fantastic shapes.

In later times, the Tudors adopted this practice, creating 'knotte-gardens' inspired by geometrical patterns in wool or silk. Labyrinths and mazes featuring low clipped hedges of lavender were especially favoured by these leisured noblefolk. They would amuse themselves for hours by playing hide-and-seek amongst the ". . . arbors and allyes so pleasant and so dulce." Parkinson wrote that ". . . the use of Germander ordinarily is as Tyme, Hyssope and other such hearbes to border a knot whereunto it is often appropriate", while Cardinal Wolsey's garden at Hampton Court was ". . . so enknotted with Lavender, it cannot be expressed."

Plan your lavender garden or nook, using the following ideas:-

φ Build a specially raised bed of brick or stone and set a

Lavender Spike hath many stiff branches of a woody sub-stance . . . the floures grow at the top of the branches, spike fashion, of a blew colour.

The Herball, John Gerard, 1597

seat in the side where the lavender is planted—thus, the aroma is at nose level.

φ Plant a display, using a mixture of purple lavenders, or alternate plants of the mauve, pink and white forms in a pattern.

φ Leave narrow borders and paths round your lavender and accent the bushes with shrub roses or other silver-leaved herbs, such as sage, santolina and curry plant. Pinks, pansies and other low-growing flowers could also be used at the edges of the path—they are pretty if allowed to grow over the edges.

φ Fill the paths with mauve-coloured pebbles, as was the fashion in Tudor times, or plant with low-growing chamomile. Place a favourite stone bird bath or sundial nearby to attract feathered friends.

φ Create a variety of different scents—plant lavender with aromatic bergamot, pelargonium, orange thyme and rosemary for a spicy effect; or, for a sweetly-scented bed, lavender complements English wallflowers, daphne, night-scented stock and violets equally well.

φ Where space is very limited, plant a lavender wheel with a 'rim' and 'spokes' of brick, tiles or wood, each segment planted with a different variety.

φ Plant double or even triple lavender hedges, with high bushes at the back and dwarf varieties in front. These can be quite spectacular, particularly if you choose varieties that bloom at different times so the flowers open in succession and attract bees through summer.

φ Tubs or large terracotta pots filled with lavender make an attractive feature on patios and balconies. Wooden barrels, cut in half and treated with wood preservative, can also be used.

φ Plant lavender, chamomile and peppermint in a hanging basket and place it by the barbeque area, or in that special spot where you sit on a warm, balmy night. The aroma will help to repel insects.

Green Magic

Through time, many gardeners have indulged a fancy for improving their lavender crops with a little white magic. If your 'green thumb' could do with some help, read on:-

φ Elizabethan gardeners were wont to steep lavender seeds in sweetened milk before sowing them, in the hope of growing an even more fragrant variety.

φ American Ozark farmers, who plant and harvest according to zodiacal lore, advise that lavender be propagated during Virgo's ascendant. Often depicted carrying a posy of blossoms, she is said to encourage the growth of all flowers.

φ Though Culpeper deemed lavender to be under the dominion of wing-footed Mercury, the fastest of the planets, it has nonetheless a peaceful domain ruling the witty and versatile Gemini and the modest diligent Virgo. Mystic botanists held that "the . . . floures would dooble if planted when Mercury was aligned with the Sunne".

φ For best results, lavender should only be pruned when the moon is waxing, never when it is waning, or the bush will wither completely.

φ Henry VIII's gardener customarily left a lavender branch uncut at pruning times 'to cherish the sap'— a folk memory of appeasing the bush's spirit for such disrespectful interference.

φ In Germany, fragments of the charred Yule log would be scattered by lavender bushes. Flattered, the bush would be encouraged to produce a good crop of flowers the next season.

φ Louisiana gardeners say whenever you give a lavender cutting or plant 'with a good heart' it will grow. For success, cuttings should always be struck in threes, perhaps in recollection of the Holy Trinity.

φ For centuries, gardeners have regarded lavender as 'a good companion', repelling all fly pests, millipedes and some slugs. Plant it by tomatoes, cabbages and carrots to encourage good crops.

An old wives' tale has it that primulas and yellow crocus—elsewhere ruined by birds—are left untouched growing beside a lavender hedge. Similarly, William Coles in 'The Art of Simpling' (1656), wrote '. . . among strawberries sow here and there some Lavender and you shall find the strawberries under those leaves fayre more layer than their fellowes.'

φ Bavarian farmers have a notion that elves are very fond of lavender. In order that they may be good-humoured and bless the cattle with sweet milk, they are careful to tie a bunch of the flowers between each cow's horns.

Harvesting

Lavender is still sometimes cut by hand in the French Alps, where farmers use specially curved hand-sickles. Elsewhere, the harvesting of lavender is mechanised and with up-to-date methods lavender is cut and distilled immediately in the field, in mobile steam distillation columns, to avoid the loss of the fragrant volatile oil. Lavender water is then made by diluting this essential oil with alcohol and combining it with other ingredients, such as bergamot.

Commercial harvesting is carried out rapidly—in a week, if possible. The bulk of the blossoms are used to make refined oil and the balance of the crop is prepared for market, being spread out on drying trays in a closed shed on the farm.

Culpeper said that ". . . as for the time of gathering flowers, let it be when the sun shines upon them, so they may be dry, for if you gather them when they be wet or dewy, they will not keep." To harvest your own lavender crop, choose a dry, sunny day and cut after the dew has dried but before the sun is at its strongest. Ideally, they should be cut just before the flower buds open, as it is then their scent and flavour are strongest.

Best among all good plants for hot sandy soils are the ever blessed Lavender and Rosemary, delicious old garden bushes that one can hardly dissociate.

Miss Gertrude Jekyll
Home and Garden, 1900

The wholesome sage and lavender
 still gray
The roses reigning in the pride of
 May
Fair marigolds and bees alluring
 thyme
Sweet marjoram and daysies in
 their prime
Colde lettuce and refreshing
 rosemarie
And whatso else of vertue, good
 or ill
Grow in this garden, fetched from
 far away
Of everyone, he takes and tastes
 at will.

Edmund Spenser
The Fate of the Butterfly, 1590

Use sharp scissors to avoid damaging the plants. Try to shape the bush at the same time so it will grow evenly—cutting the central spikes will cause the side shoots to grow quickly if you are trying to encourge a hedge. Unless you are pruning and tidying at the same time, pick only as much lavender as you can deal with in one day. Discard any blemished or discoloured sprigs and handle the leaves as little as possible. Take the lavender indoors immediately after cutting.

Depending on the size of your harvest, bunch the lavender with fine cotton string and hang it in a dark cupboard to dry, or spread it on drying frames. These may be simply prepared from light wood, each one strengthened with a diagonal cross-piece, with hessian or muslin stretched over them. Care must be taken to ensure the stems do not touch, for they will be spoilt by the dampness engendered. Keep in a dark airy room where the temperature does not exceed 30°C. Wait until flowers are completely dry. They should crackle crisply, or they may reabsorb moisture and become musty.

A quicker method is oven drying. Set the oven at 50°C. Place the lavender on brown paper on the oven racks and poke a few slits in the paper to increase air movement. Leave the oven door open to allow moisture to escape. Turn the flowers regularly, until crisp and dry. Microwaves are marvellous for drying lavender, and have the added bonus of helping the flowers to keep their shape and colour.

If you are not planning to use your lavender immediately, it is best to store it in an airtight, light-proof container until you are ready. The scent will remain strong for 6–8 months and any lavender left can be added to the compost heap, scattered on your herb garden or sprinkled round pot plants.

The distilled water of Lavender cleareth the sight and putteth away all spottes, lentils, freckles and redness of the face if they be often washed therewith.

The Herball, by John Gerard, 1597

Preparation

Fresh or dried lavender is generally made into a liquid preparation—most commonly, a maceration, infusion or decoction.

Infusions and decoctions of lavender are made like ordinary tea. The chopped fresh or crumbled dry flowers are put into a pot, covered with boiling water and left to brew for a given period. The liquid is strained and drunk hot, or cooled and combined with other ingredients for cosmetic or medicinal use.

A maceration consists of sprigs of fresh lavender steeped in alcohol or oil for some days, and then strained before use. Lavender oil, lavender honey and lavender vinegar are all easy-to-prepare macerations. For the vinegar, steep flowers in a bottle of white vinegar on a sunny window sill for three weeks. Jasmine flowers and rose leaves may also be included. Strain before use. To prepare lavender oil, substitute fine almond or olive oil for the vinegar and follow the same steps. Delicious and aromatic honey may be made by covering the flowers with clear honey and kirsch. Leave for six weeks before use.

Lavender Cuisine

To Candy All Kinds of Flowers In Wayes of Spanish Candy

Take double refined sugar, put it into a posnet with as much rose-water as will melt it, and put into it the pappe of half a roasted apple, and a grain of musk, then let it boyl till it come to a candy height, then put in your flowers being picked, and so let it boyl, then cast them on a fine plate, and cut inwayes with your knife, then you may spot it with gold and keep it.

A Choice Manual of Secrets, by Elizabeth Grey, Countess of Kent, 1653

Lavender's warm, evocative smell made it a favourite herb for strewing and it was scattered over banqueting tables to sweeten the air and sharpen jaded appetites.

The use of lavender flowers in, and as, food, was once widespread. Coles wrote in 1656 that they ". . . do comfort the wearied braine with fragrant smells which yield a certayne kind of nourishment." Lavender was crystallised for eating as a sweetmeat, used for decorating fruit dishes and included in jellies and jams. In fact, Elizabeth I delighted in lavender conserve, and used it liberally as a relish. Lavender was also used to mask the gamey taste of ill-preserved meat. The French continue to send their baby lambs to graze in fields of lavender, so their meat will be tender and fragrant.

The powdered flowers are found in some Provencal compound spices under the Moroccan name 'khzame' and in their dish, ras-el-hanout. Also, very old French recipes for pâté mention 'spic', being *L. spica*. However, lavender is best known as an ambrosial accompaniment to all summer fruits, salads and cocktails. Light dishes, such as flans, cakes, desserts and jellies are all improved by a few lavender flowers, and it is pleasant in pork or chicken stuffing, too. Mixed

Conserve of the Flowers of Lavender
Take the flowers being new so many as you please, and beat them with three times their weight of White Sugar, after the same manner as Rosemary flowers; they will keep one year.

The Queen's Closet Opened
by W.M., Cook to Queen
Henrietta Maria, 1655

with vinegar and poured over orange segments, lavender is a delicious complement to roast duck; or, try a lavender sauce over rabbit.

Lavender may be used in quite delightful ways to decorate and present foods. Freshen your table with some new ideas.

- Decorate an immaculate white linen napkin, on which a terrine or pâté is displayed, with two or three lavender flowers.

- Prepare a summer dessert platter, skewering sweets and small chunks of fresh fruit with lavender stems.

- Scatter lavender heads through a sweet salad of walnuts, currants and cos lettuce; toss with Lavender Vinegar.

- Make lavender ice cubes by putting one flower and a little grated lemon rind in each compartment of an ice tray, covering with lavender water. Pop into a pitcher of chilled wine or fruit punch.

- Weave a wreath of pink and mauve lavender flowers and place it around the rim of a bowl containing chocolate mousse.

- Icing a special sponge cake? Combine equal parts of icing sugar and softened butter with finely chopped lavender. Intensify the colour with a few drops of purple food colouring.

- Decorate soft desserts with fresh or crystallised lavender-grape jelly, caramel pudding and creamy blancmanges, for instance.

- Infuse lavender flowers in double cream and use strained liquid to make custards and creamy desserts, such as rice pudding and syllabubs. Whipped and hot, it makes a luscious topping for fruit pies or scones.

- Crumble a handful of lavender flowers over soft white cheese before serving with water-crackers.

- Add lavender flowers to fresh fruit punch and use crystallised buds to trim the glasses.

Aunt Jobiska made him drink lavender water tinged with pink
For she said 'The World in general knows
There's nothing so good for a Pobble's toes!'

Edward Lear
The Pobble with No Toes, 1846

Recipes

A few tips when selecting lavender for food preparation. Firstly, avoid blooms that have been sprayed with pesticides. Choose flowers that are free of blemishes and, of course, insects. Gently shake each lavender spike with its head downwards to dislodge unwelcome visitors. Gather flowers after the dew has disappeared and before the sun gets too hot, for this is when they will have the most fragrance and flavour. If your lavender needs to be washed, do so gently—few recipes will be improved by waterlogged flowers.

———— LAVENDER CONFECTIONERY ————

LAVENDER SUGAR

This adds a new dimension to sweet dishes, and is especially lovely when dusted over summer fruits still fresh with morning dew. Substitute lavender sugar for ordinary sugar when preparing puddings or creamy desserts, and add it to whipped cream or plain boiled custard.

10 lavender flowers
caster sugar
lavender essence

Combine sugar and lavender flowers and place in cannister; seal. Add lavender essence for beautifully scented sugar.

CRYSTALLISED LAVENDER

Use as a garnish when decorating sweet dishes and cakes.

lavender flowers and leaves
1 egg white, lightly whisked
caster sugar

Pat flowers dry with absorbent paper to remove dew or moisture. Paint flowers and leaves on both sides with egg white. Dust with caster sugar and place on greaseproof paper in a slow oven for ten minutes, or until crisp.

LAVENDER TOFFEE

Simple to make, toffee is an old-fashioned favourite at chidren's parties and school fêtes. If it is to be for gifts or prizes, wrap each piece in purple or green cellophane.

20 lavender flowers, finely chopped
500g caster sugar
100ml water
pinch cream of tartar
1 tsp apple cider vinegar

Grease a shallow tin with butter. Place all ingredients in a saucepan and heat until boiling. Mixture should clarify after about 10 minutes, i.e., it will look like clear honey. Remove from heat and pour into tin. As mixture cools, mark surface into squares with a sharp knife.

LAVENDER JUBES

Just the thing to serve with sweet sherry at twilight-time . . .

20 lavender flowers, finely chopped
500g sugar
250ml water
30g gelatine
cochineal, icing sugar, lemon juice

Combine sugar and lavender. Add half the water to the gelatine; leave for half an hour. Put all ingredients in saucepan, adding lemon juice and cochineal to taste. Pour into slightly wetted moulds. Chill and dust lightly with icing sugar. Top each jube with a crystallised lavender bud.

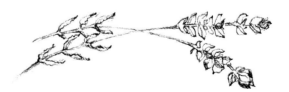

... a pleasant and efficacious cordial and very useful in langour and weakness of the nerves, lowness of spirits, faintings, etc.

Mrs M Grieve
A Modern Herbal, 1931

LAVENDER BEVERAGES

LAVENDER TEA

In 1824, Henry Phillips wrote that '. . . many persons prefer the infusion of these leaves to the tea of China'.

Lavender tea is calming and refreshing, as it does not contain the caffeine present in ordinary tea and coffee. In summer, chill lavender tea and add a little honey for a delicious iced drink. Don't forget that picking lavender for your tea-pot is itself a relaxing occupation. Experiment with flavours—chamomile, lavender and bergamot are a very pleasant combination.

6 lavender flowers
water
lavender sugar or lavender honey to taste

Infuse the flowers in boiling water and leave to draw for five minutes.

LAVENDER LEMON TEA

A soothing tea with a light, fresh taste, exquisite aroma and the added bonus of rapidly easing a headache. Make a pretty gift for a friend by packing Lavender Lemon Tea into a tin and placing one dried flower spike on top of the mixture before sealing.

6 lavender flowers
1 tbsp dried lemon rind
water
lavender sugar or lavender honey to taste

Combine flowers and rind in tea-pot. Pour boiling water over and steep for five minutes before pouring into warmed china cups.

No man need doubt the wholesomeness of Ale, being brewed as it should be with Sage, Rosemary, Betony, Scabious, Lavender . . . and Fennel Seed.

The Herball, by John Gerard, 1579

LAVENDER CHAMPAGNE

Delicious and heady, pour lavender-scented champagne into chilled flutes, dipping the rim of each glass in lavender sugar before serving.

40 lavender flowers
2.25 litres water
325g sugar
110g sultanas, finely chopped
2 tbspns white wine vinegar
juice of 1 lemon

Combine all ingredients. Place lavender in large, non-metallic pot and add liquid. Cover with lid and leave for one week. Strain and pour into warm, sterilised bottles and cap securely. At the end of the following week, liquid should be effervescent.

LAVENDER LIQUEUR

Drink this delicious and unusual liqueur as an after dinner digestive, or as a mixer with vermouth. Or, drizzle it over fruit and creamy desserts.

40 lavender flowers
100g rose petals
1 tsp coriander
1 tsp aniseed
pinch licorice powder
brandy

Pack all ingredients into a bottle and cover with brandy. Seal and store in a cool, dark place for 6 months, shaking occasionally. Strain and decant into cut glass liqueur bottle. For a charming gift, paint a spray of lavender on the front of a bottle and pour the liqueur into it. Trim the neck of the bottle with ribbon and card.

NUTTY LAVENDER NOG

This soothing and delicious beverage is a marvellous restorative for a patient with a sore throat or a feverish child.

30 lavender flowers, bruised
250ml milk
2 eggs, separated
lavender sugar
nutmeg or allspice
1 tbspn ground almond meal

Heat milk to simmering and infuse lavender for 15 minutes; strain. Beat egg yolks, almond meal and sugar together and add to milk. Whisk egg whites till frothy and fold through. Sprinkle with spice and serve immediately.

LAVENDER FRUIT CUP

A delicately flavoured and fragrant drink, perfect for poolside entertaining.

20 lavender flowers
400ml orange juice
400ml ginger ale
200ml dry vermouth
juice of 1 lemon
punnet of small strawberries
sprig of lemon thyme

Rub base of punch bowl with lavender before adding all liquid and hulled, sliced stawberries. Chill for 30 minutes before serving.

Lavender drying in an armoire

Plant lavender around garden ornaments

LAVENDER CORDIAL

Diluted with hot water, this cordial is ideal for soothing a sore throat or cough. In summer, add it to sparkling mineral water for a refreshing treat.

40 lavender flowers
300ml water
100g sugar

Dissolve sugar in water, bring to boil and infuse flowers for 20 minutes. Strain. Re-heat liquid, stirring constantly until syrupy consistency is reached. Pour into sterile bottle, cap securely and refrigerate.

LAVENDER CONSERVES

Lavender sauces and spreads are fun to make, keep well in a jar and make delightful gifts.

LAVENDER AND GINGER JAM

40 lavender flowers
5 green apples, peeled cored and chopped
425g sugar
350ml water
150ml dry sherry
125g jellied ginger root
2 tsp ground ginger
1 lemon, rind and juice

Simmer apples in water till soft. Add lavender, ground ginger and lemon juice. Boil rapidly. Add sugar and jellied ginger and boil until mixture thickens. Cool and strain. Pour into sterile jars—a pretty touch is to add a few lavender buds before securing lid.

LAVENDER AND ALMOND BUTTER

This is particularly delightful on scones, fruit buns, sweet biscuits and pancakes.

10 lavender flowers, chopped
125g unsalted butter
2 tbspn ground almond meal
1 tbspn caster sugar
brandy and almond essence to taste

Blend all ingredients until mixture is smooth and fluffy. Spoon into small glass dish and refrigerate before serving.

The young and tender sproutings are kept in pickle and reserved to be eaten with meat, as Dioscorides teacheth.

The Herball, by John Gerard, 1597

LAVENDER SPREAD

An unusual and flavoursome dip. Serve with a wicker basket containing chunks of crusty, homemade bread.

20 lavender flowers, chopped
200g cottage or ricotta cheese
juice of 1 large lemon
a little cayenne or paprika

Blend all ingredients till smooth. Spoon into small earthenware pot and chill before serving.

LAVENDER AND MUSTARD SEED CHUTNEY

This spicy pickle goes well with all meat dishes. Or try serving it with soft white cheese and plain cracker biscuits.

20 lavender flowers, chopped
2 tbspn mustard seed
3 lemons
3 onions, diced
60g sultanas
cinnamon stick
allspice and sugar, to taste
apple cider vinegar

Chop lemons into small pieces and remove pips. Place in a mixing bowl and sprinkle with salt. Cover with apple cider vinegar and let stand for 24 hours. Place lemons in saucepan and add remaining ingredients. Bring to boil, then cover and simmer till lemon pieces are well softened and liquid is reduced. Remove cinnamon stick. Pour chutney into sterile jars and cap securely.

LAVENDER BREAD

A tasty complement to these conserves comes from Mrs Judy Stephenson in Victoria, Australia—easy to make, too!

½ cup English lavender
3 cups wholemeal flour
3 cups white flour
2 cups hot water
2 tspn salt
2 tspn oil
2 tspn dried yeast
I tspn sugar
125g vitamin C tablet, crushed

Combine yeast, vitamin C, sugar and hot water in a bowl; let stand for five minutes. Combine flours and add slowly to mix along with oil, salt and lavender. Knead and leave dough to rise in a plastic bag for 30 mins. Knock down and knead again. Shape and place in bread tin, cover with plastic and leave to rise again. Cook for 30 mins at 220°C.

LAVENDER VINEGAR

A delicious and aromatic alternative to the traditional mint sauce which accompanies the Sunday roast. Also, try using Lavender Vinegar in salad dressings.

20 lavender flowers, bruised
375ml apple cider vinegar
I tbspn lavender honey
I tbspn black peppercorns
I tsp allspice

Combine all ingredients in a lidded jar. Steep on a sunny windowsill for two weeks, shaking vigorously every day. Strain and decant liquid into sterile glass bottle; cap securely.

LAVENDER HONEY DRESSING

A tangy smooth dressing, perfect for a crisp green salad.

40 lavender flowers, bruised
2 tbspns fresh parsley
2 tspns fresh rosemary
50g raw honey
4 cloves garlic
150ml apple cider vinegar
150ml olive oil
pinch curry powder

Blend all ingredients, except olive oil, at high speed in food processor. Stir olive oil through mixture and shake well just before serving.

LAVENDER DESSERTS

LAVENDER SORBET

A refreshing summertime dessert—to create a splendid centrepiece for a party, serve sorbet in an ice mould. Simply arrange flowers in ring mould, add water and freeze. Decant onto serving platter and heap scoops of sorbet in the centre.

20 lavender flowers
200ml champagne
200ml water
175g sugar
1 large egg white
juice of 1 lemon

Dissolve sugar in water and champagne. Bring to boil and infuse flowers for 30 minutes. Add lemon juice, strain, and pour into metal freezer tray. Chill until mixture begins to freeze, then fold through whisked egg white. Freeze again till firm.

PEACHY LAVENDER ICE CREAM

Garnished with crystallised lavender and fresh peach slices, this is a delicious finale to a special dinner party.

20 lavender flowers, chopped
250g canned peaches, strained
150g caster sugar
4 egg yolks, beaten
350ml double cream

Mash sugar, chopped lavender flowers and peaches with egg yolks in saucepan. Stir over low heat, adding cream gradually until mixture forms a custardy coating on a metal spoon. Remove from heat, pour into bowl and chill until it begins to freeze. Remove from freezer. Beat vigorously until smooth and creamy. Pour into tray and freeze.

LAVENDER PUDDING

10 lavender flowers
300ml milk
300ml double cream
4 tbspns rice
50g lavender sugar
4 tsp ground pecan nuts

Infuse flowers in milk for 15 minutes; strain. Combine sugar, rice and nuts. Add milk slowly over a gentle flame, stirring until mixture thickens. Add half the cream, pour into dessert bowls and refrigerate. Whip the remaining cream and pipe around bowls. Decorate with crystallised lavender buds.

LAVENDER AND RHUBARB PIE

20 lavender flowers, chopped
100g rhubarb, coarsely chopped
30g flaked almonds
grated zest of grapefruit
4 tbspn lavender sugar
4 sheets frozen short pastry
pinch allspice

Simmer lavender flowers with rhubarb, sugar, grapefruit zest, almonds and allspice until fruit has softened. Strain mixture. Line pie dish with pastry, and spoon mix evenly over it. Cover with extra pastry sheet and decorate with almonds. Bake in a moderate oven for 20–25 minutes.

LAVENDER FRUIT DELIGHT

Complement fresh summer fruit with the warm fragrance and rich colour of lavender.

10 lavender flowers
kiwi fruit, sliced
rockmelon or honeydew, chopped
seedless green grapes
gooseberries
currants
mango, sliced

Toss salad with Kirsch and a little lime juice. Top with whipped Lavender Cream.

LAVENDER PANCAKES

10 lavender flowers, chopped
100g plain flour
100ml sweet white wine
2 apples, pureed
40g melted butter
2 egg whites, beaten
1 tsp lavender sugar
pinch each salt and baking soda

Combine sifted flour, sugar, salt, soda and lavender. Add wine, apple puree and egg whites, stirring to form a smooth batter. leave for 1 hour, then fold through butter. Fry spoonfuls of batter in pan, turning rapidly till crisp at the edges. Serve with caster sugar and lemon.

Lavender for Milady

The Egyptians used lavender oil ". . . to drive away sweaty feet in a person", and in preparing the white wax cones worn atop their ornate wigs—as the wax melted, the scent drizzled over their shoulders. Marie Antoinette rubbed her teeth with lavender flowers and sage leaves to give them a silky fresh feel. Her contemporary, the notorious courtesan Ninon de Lenclos, dusted her hair with lavender powder and ordered tiny organza sachets of the flowers be stitched inside all her wigs and hats.

Lavender has long been cultivated for its scent. In his *Livre des Parfums* of 1864, Eugene Rimmel described it as ". . . a nice clean scent and an old and deserving favourite". Commercial perfume houses still use it as the basic ingredient of many fragrances and as a nuancer for cologne, chypre and leather types. In addition, its soothing antiseptic and anti-inflammatory properties mean this well-loved flower may be used to make a variety of cosmetic aids.

For instance, lavender is an effective mouthwash, skin tonic and eye lotion, helping to treat mild infection or irritation, eg: cuts, insect bites and fungal infections. Try an infusion in the bath to heal skin troubled with a rash.

This plant is very useful to the Ladies and ought to be found upon their toilets. Its decoction will take away freckles which are brought on by the heat of the Sunne. It is so innocent . . . no harm need by feared from its application.

The English Physitian or an Astrologo-Physical Discourse by the Vulgar Herbs of this Nation . . ., by Nicolas Culpeper, 1653

To scent the skin and stimulate the circulation, combine lavender with other scented oils from its own plant family, such as marjoram and rosemary. The essence also blends well with rose, geranium and thyme.

Lavender helps to regenerate skin cells and is thus excellent for burns—especially sunburn—and chapping. Also, by balancing the activity of the sebaceous glands, lavender will tone oily skin and help to treat acne. If you are plagued by a nasty pimple, take a cotton bud and dab it firstly in camphor, then in lavender oil, before applying directly to the blemish. This will often clear the culprit overnight.

Skin Care and Cleansing

LAVENDER YOGHURT CLEANSER

This recipe is particularly effective for adolescents, and those with oily skin.

20 lavender flowers
150ml water
150g natural yoghurt

Pour boiling water over lavender and infuse; cool and strain. Blend lavender water with yoghurt. Massage gently into skin, before rinsing off with cool water.

LAVENDER ANTISEPTIC WASH

A gentle astringent lotion for those troubled with pimply blemishes or acne, this recipe will help balance the skin's acid mantle and refine large pores.

20 lavender flowers
250ml apple cider vinegar
50ml witch hazel
5 drops oil of juniper

Mix all ingredients in a lidded jar and steep on a sunny windowsill for two weeks, shaking thoroughly each day. Strain, and apply to affected area with moistened cotton ball.

TRADITIONAL LAVENDER BATH BAGS

Lavender has long been used as an aromatic bath herb ". . . to beautifie and cleanse the skinne", according to Gerard. Rather than putting lavender directly into the bathtub—where it will stick to your skin and clog up the plug hole—it is better to spoon your herb mixture into a bath bag and add it to the bath as the water is running. Be sure to spoil yourself as you soak in the bath. Put a pillow behind your shoulders and have a large soft towel ready to dry yourself with.

20 lavender flowers
1 tbspn chamomile flowers
2 tbspn bran
towelling face cloth

Place all ingredients in the centre of the cloth. Gather up the sides to make a pouch and secure firmly with ribbon. Before getting in, wet the bag and squeeze it to release the milky bran and lavender essence. Use the bag to scrub yourself gently all over, thus softening and perfuming the skin.

LAVENDER WASH BALLS

The Tudor court bathed in floral toilet waters, washing themselves with balls made from powdered soap and grated herbs or barks. These acted more like pumice stones than the smooth soap we know today—nonetheless, they make a pretty gift.

2 tbspn lavender flowers, crushed and dried
1 tbspn rose petals, crushed and dried
75g Castile soap, grated
125ml rose-water
lavender essential oil
mauve or pink vegetable colouring

Melt soap and combine with rose-water over a low flame, stirring with a wooden spoon. Cool slightly then add oil. Roll into balls and leave in the sun on a piece of greaseproof paper for about two hours. Wet your hands with a little more rose-water and polish each ball till smooth. Leave to dry completely overnight.

Take a Quarter of a Pound of Calamus Aromaticus, a Quarter of a Pound of Lavender Flowers, six Ounces of Orris, two Ounces of Rose Leaves, and an ounce of Cypres; pownd all these together in a Mortar, and rub them through a fine Sieve, then scrape Castile soap and dissolve it in Rose-water, put in your beaten Powder, pownd it in a Mortar and make it up into Balls.

From *The Receipt Book of John Nott, Cook to the Duke of Bolton, 1723*

LAVENDER SOAP

Rinsing away grime and smoothing the skin with a deliciously-scented cake of lavender soap must definitely be one of life's pleasures! Try making heart-shaped lavender soaps—wrapped in mauve tulle and tied with green ribbon, they make a lovely gift.

10 lavender flowers
1 cake plain Castile soap
55ml water

Infuse lavender in boiling water for half an hour. Strain and pour into double saucepan. Grate the soap and add slowly to infusion over low heat, stirring constantly till mixture is thoroughly combined. Press mixture firmly into slightly wetted mould and top with a spray of flowers. Leave to harden for two days.

LAVENDER FACIAL MASK

If you are bothered by age spots or freckles, this mask will help bleach them as it gently firms the skin and draws out impurities.

3 tsp lavender infusion
1 egg white
1 tsp honey
1/2 tsp almond oil
juice of 1 lemon

Whisk all ingredients through blender and then brush liquid onto clean damp skin, avoiding eye area. Lie down for ten to fifteen minutes and allow mask to dry, before rinsing off gently.

INVIGORATING LAVENDER SCRUB

Simple to make, this scrub will bring a healthy glow to sallow skin. Lavender's antiseptic properties help heal any infection and reduce inflammation.

20 lavender flowers
3 tsp fresh parsley
50g almond meal

Delicate Wash-Balls—Take four Ounces of the Flowers of Lavender, 4 Ounces of Calamus Aromaticus, 2 Ounces of Rose Leaves, 2 Ounces of Cypress, and 6 Ounces of Orris; pound all these together in a Mortar, then searse them through a fine searse, then having scraped a sufficient quantity of Castile soap, dissolve it in Rose-Water, mix the Powder with them, beat and blend well them together, in a Mortar, then make them up into Balls.

The Receipt Book of Charles Carter
Cook to the Duke of Argyll, 1732

50g Fullers Earth
150ml water

Infuse the lavender and parsley in boiling water for half an hour. Cool, strain and mix liquid with almond meal and Fullers Earth to form a paste. Apply to slightly damp skin with light, circular movements. Rinse with lukewarm water and pat dry.

LAVENDER BUBBLE BATH

This gel is ideal for cleaning up a troupe of grubby small children, with the added bonus of disinfecting any little nicks or grazes they may have collected whilst playing.

20 lavender flowers, minced
200g flaked Castile soap
150ml boiling water
oil of lavender

Blend soap and water in a saucepan over a low heat. Stir through lavender and add oil as desired. Leave to stand at room temperature until gel-like consistency is reached. Spoon into sterilised jar, and cap securely.

TONING

Rinsing the complexion with sweet lavender water, especially that made from rain or spring water, has long been believed to beautify the skin. Such waters were once kept in elegant silver ewers in fine ladies' bed-chambers.

LAVENDER FLOWER BALM

Use this freshening lotion to whisk away the last traces of make-up, soap or grime which can dull the skin.

1 tbspn lavender infusion
1 tbspn chamomile infusion
1 tbspn elderflower infusion
100ml rose-water

Place all ingredients in a lidded glass jar and shake well before applying with moistened cotton ball.

LAVENDER AND ROSEMARY TONER

A mildly astringent preparation which helps close the pores and refine the texture of the skin, leaving the face feeling fresh and ready for the application of moisturiser.

20 lavender flowers
2 tbspns rosemary leaves
125ml witch hazel
125ml water
3 drops peppermint oil

Infuse herbs for five minutes and leave to cool. Strain, pressing down well on flowers, and add peppermint oil. Decant into an atomiser or glass-stoppered bottle.

MOISTURISING

Lavender has long been a valuable ingredient in moisturising lotions and creams, both for its fragrance and for its stimulating effect upon the skin cells.

LAVENDER NOURISHING NIGHT CREAM

This is an excellent regenerative treatment and particularly appropriate for dry or mature skin. Lavish it on elbows, knees or roughened hands to soften and smooth. Also very good for sunburnt shoulders and noses.

1 tsp oil of lavender
2 tbpsn beeswax
2 tbspn lanolin
2 tbspn olive oil
1 tsp almond oil

Combine all ingredients in a double saucepan, stirring constantly till melted. Pour in sterilised glass pot; cool, and cap securely.

This recipe may be adapted for use on an oily complexion by replacing the lanolin and olive oil measures with plain yoghurt and cider vinegar.

LAVENDER & HONEY SKIN REPAIR

The combination of lavender's antiseptic properties with gentle honey and the time-honoured healing herb, comfrey, make this cream invaluable for soothing sunburn or chafing.

1 tsp lavender infusion
1 tsp lavender oil
1 tsp comfrey root powder
3 tbspns honey
3 tbspns white beeswax
2 tbspns almond oil

Melt honey, beeswax and almond oil together in a double saucepan, stirring constantly. Add comfrey, lavender infusion and oil. Pour into lidded glass jar and shake well.

EXTRA-RICH LAVENDER OIL

This recipe works wonders on rough or chapped hands, and will help heal any nicks, split cuticles or bruises. Gardeners take note!—apply to your hands, then don an old pair of cotton gloves before putting on your heavy gardening gloves.

1 tsp lavender oil
1 tsp raw honey
1 tbspn glycerine and rosewater
2 tbspn sesame oil
2 tbspn almond oil

Melt honey in double saucepan, then whisk together with oils and glycerine. Pour into sterile glass jar and cap securely.

LAVENDER AND LIME FLOWER MASSAGE OIL

1 handful each dried lavender flowers and lime flowers
200ml avocado oil
100ml apple cider vinegar

Pack flowers into glass jar and cover with oil. Leave in a cool, dark place for three weeks, shaking occasionally. Heat the mixture, strain flowers off and add apple cider vinegar. Pour into sterile jar and cool before capping.

LAVENDER FOOT CREAM

Tired feet make a tired-looking face. Pay your tootsies some attention, and perk them up with a fabulous foot massage. Start at the toes and work up to your ankles and calves. Massage gently but firmly, paying special attention to the reflex zones under the arch of the foot and between the toes. After massage, rest and relax them for ten minutes, lying with your feet raised above your head.

6 tbspn oil of lavender
25ml almond oil
3 tbspn lanolin
3 tbspn glycerine

Combine all ingredients in a double saucepan, stirring constantly till evenly blended. Pour into sterile lidded jar.

Hair Care

Lavender is very good for the hair. It may be dabbed directly onto the scalp to ease irritation, flaking or dandruff. Or, include the oil in an everyday hair conditioner to help balance oil secretion.

LAVENDER HAIR RINSE

Use this as a final aromatic rinse after shampooing. It will envelop you in a soft, romantic cloud of fragrance, with the added bonus of help to offset any scalp dryness or flyaway hair after shampooing.

20 lavender flowers
1 tbspn clary sage oil
250ml apple cider vinegar
50ml whisky.

Combine all ingredients in a lidded jar and steep for two weeks. Strain and re-bottle.

Enjoy a lavender oil massage after your bath

Victorian lavender garland

LAVENDER HAIR GLOSS

This recipe leaves hair wonderfully smooth and shiny.

25ml lavender oil
150ml clear honey
30g clear henna wax

Melt all ingredients together and comb paste through hair. Sit out in the sun and allow to dry, then rinse out thoroughly with warm water.

LAVENDER HAIR TONIC

A stimulating massage treatment for scalp and hair problems, especially dandruff. Diluted, this recipe will also help clear up cradle cap in babies.

5 drops of oil of lavender
10 drops oil of bay
5 drops tea-tree oil, or eucalyptus
150ml pure alcohol
150ml castor oil

Mix all oils together. Warm, and massage gently into scalp.

Fragrance

No chapter on the cosmetic uses of lavender would be complete without mentioning its use as a perfume. Lavender water, as it is made today, cannot compare with the old methods such as this 19th receipt from Sir Joseph Swan for "The distiling of Lavender":-

The juice boiled in old oil takes away roughness of the skin, scurf, or dry scabs in the head or other parts, if they be anointed with the decoction, and preserve the hair from falling off.

The English Physitian or an Astrologo-Physical Discourse of the Vulgar Herbs of this Nation, by Nicolas Culpeper, 1653

"A pound of flowers stripped of their stems is packed into a quart crock. Pour over compound spirit made from 3 pounds Essence of Spike, 1 pound Spirit of Rosemary, ½ ounce Cinnamon, ½ ounce Nutmeg and 3 drachms Red Saunders. Heat the quart crock in a saucepan of water and keep it boiling till the essence has come; it will make about 7½ ounces, but will be better than anything you cay buy."

LAVENDER TOILET WATER

You may like to try making this simple, delicate scent yourself, using freshly picked flowers from your garden.

40 lavender flowers
1 tbspn rose geranium leaves
1 tbspn lemon verbena leaves
2 tspn grated orange rind
2 tbspn brandy
500ml water

Pour water over flowers and leaves. Cover and steep for two days. Chill, strain and stir brandy through mixture. Store in an atomiser and keep in the fridge for a refreshing spritz on a hot day.

Lavender Beauty Tips

φ Steep lavender flowers and cloves in water. Gargle daily with the liquid to keep breath sweet and cleanse the mouth and tongue.

φ A sovereign remedy for perspiration odour is to dab 1 drop of lavender essence under each arm. Or combine lemon juice, oil of lavender and witch hazel in a pump atomiser and use for natural freshness, every day.

φ If you must wear close-fitting shoes, sprinkle a powder made from dried lavender flowers and peppermint leaves inside them to check odour and perspiration.

φ A compress soaked with a strong infusion of lavender and marigold oil will help ease redness or blisters on heels.

φ An elegant party look, especially suitable for a girl with dark hair. Slick hair back to nape of neck with a smidgin of lavender oil. Tuck a spray of the purple flowers into the chignon, or twist buds into a wreath made of florist's wire with a little maidenhair fern.

To Make Sweet Water

Take Damask Roses at discretion, Basil, Sweet Marjoram, Lavender, Walnut Leafs, of each two handfuls, Rosemary one handful, a little Balm, Cloves, Cinnamon, one Ounce, Bay Leaf; Rosemary tops, Limon and Orange Pills of each a few; pour upon these as much White Wine as will conveniently wet them, and let them infuse ten or twelve days; then distil it off.

Receipts in Physick and Chirurgery,
by Sir Kenelm Digby, 1668

The distilled water of the floures of Rosemary being drunke at morning and evening first and last, taketh away the stench of the mouth and breath, and maketh it very sweet, if there is to be added thereto, to steep or infuse for certaine daies, a few Cloves, Mace, Spike, Cinnamon and a little Annise Seed.

The Herball, by John Gerard, 1597

φ   If hair is very brittle, combine rosemary and lavender oil, rub several drops between the palms and pat lightly over wet hair before combing through.

φ   Massage face and neck with equal parts of lavender, rose and myrrh oils each night. This will have a tonic effect, stimulating the growth of new skin cells and improving circulation.

φ   Treat yourself to a lavender facial steam. Place a handful of lavender and a pinch of rosemary in a porcelain bowl, then cover with boiling water. With a towel over your head, lean over the fragrant steam for 10 minutes. Then splash face with cold water and pat dry. Not only does the steam eliminate oils and impurities from the skin, but it leaves you feeling relaxed and refreshed—the greatest beauty tonic of all.

Lavender Remedies

What then is called the royal unguent, because it is a blend prepared for the kings of Parthia, is made of behen-nut juice, costus, amomum, Syrian cinnamon, cardomum, nardinum, cat-thyme, myrrh, cinnamon-bark, ladanum, balm, Syrian reed and Syrian rush . . . gladiolus, marjoram, lotus, honey and wine . . .

Natural History, by
Pliny the Elder, A.D. 23-79

The treatment of disease with plants is the oldest form of medicine. Old wives used lavender to treat headaches, induce peaceful slumber, soothe sprained limbs and stimulate the digestive system after illness. Its therapeutic properties were recognised by monks, who spent many hours devoutly tending lavender hedges in their formal 'Physicke Gardens', so they might use the oil to heal their patients.

Formal study of the indications of lavender originated with the medieval Doctrine of Signatures. This treatise maintained every plant had virtues which could be deduced from its outward appearance. Thus, herbs with yellow sap, such as the Greater Celandine, would be good for jaundice and those with blue-grey flowers, such as lavender, could be used to treat bruising.

Lavender was much in demand in Tudor England, when street vendors cried:-

"Won't you buy my sweet lavender, fresh lavender
Sweet blooming lavender, who'll buy?"

The flowers were used for scenting clothes, flavouring food and as a sternutatory . . . that is, they were an ingredient

of snuff. Sugary lavender 'confects', or 'comfits', were used
to treat many complaints and Defoe, in his graphic
description of the Great Plague of London, suggested tying
a bunch of lavender to each wrist as a means of repelling
infection.

Along with garlic and cloves, lavender was an ingredient
of 'Four Thieves Vinegar'. This infamous brew was
attributed to a team of grave-robbers who preyed on plague
victims in 18th century Marseilles. Before and after stripping
the corpses of valuables, these ghouls were said to rinse their
hands and faces with the vinegar—and they survived
without contracting the disease.

By the 19th century, lavender appeared in the London
Pharmacopeia as an ingredient of "Palsy Drops", a costly
but excellent medicine which was a sovereign remedy for
". . . the Falling Sickness, and all Cold Distempers of the
Head, Womb, Stomach and Nerves; against the Apoplexy,
Palsy, Convulsions, Migrim, Vertigo, Loss of Memory,
Dimness of Sight, Melancholy, Swooning Fits and Barreness
in Women." It was given to patients diluted in "Juice of
Black Cherries, or in Florence Wine . . . in milk or faire water
sweetened with sugar."

Both orthodox and alternative health practitioners
continue to testify to lavender's therapeutic and healing
powers. In particular, aromatherapists prescribe oil of
lavender for massage, skin troubles, swollen joints, tiredness
and depression.

Lavender in the Medicine Chest

Aches   Rub any sore spots with lavender oil to reduce pain.
It has a three-way action—it reduces local pain, lowers
the central nervous system's reaction to pain and tones
the skin and lymphatic system.

Hot poultices of damp lavender seeds are useful when
applied as fomentations to relieve aches and pains. A few
drops of lavender oil in a hot footbath will have a positive

Abstersive, Aperitive, Astringent, Discursive, Diuretick, and Incisive . . . Cephalick, Neurotick, Stomatick, Cordial, Nephretick and Hysterick. It is Alexipharmick, Analeptick and Antiparatitick, being of very subtil and thin parts.

The English Herbal, by William Salmon, 1710

affect on tired, aching feet. Outwardly applied, it relieves toothache, neuralgia and sprains. Use a hot compress of the flowers.

Acne   Combined with bergamot, lavender is one of the most valuable oils for the treatment of acne. It inhibits the bacteria which cause the skin infection while soothing the skin, balancing its acidity and helping to control the over-secretion of sebum, which the bacteria thrive upon. Lavender also may be used to treat and prevent scarring.

Antiseptic   Did you know that during World War II, every English home with a lavender bush was asked to harvest the flowers and take them to the local medical supplies unit? There they were used for their powerful antiseptic properties. Try a warm poultice of damp lavender flowers to draw the pus out of an infected wound. Or use the oil in a gargle as an anti-cold remedy.

Bath   An aromatic bath with lavender will give an enormous amount of relief from muscular pain following exercise, or arising from tension. Lower back pain can be especially helped this way. Try a hot bath with a dash of juniper essence and lavender oil to help ward off a cold and stimulate the circulation.

Bleeding and Cuts   Use lavender tincture or tea, or the whole crushed flowers as a warm poultice, to stem bleeding and clean a wound. For a child's grazed knees or gravel rash, use a few drops of lavender oil in cool boiled water to wash the wound. This will reduce stiffness and speed healing.

Lavandula . . . hast a flour sundel blew . . . the vertu of this herbe is ef it be sothyn in water and dronke that water is wele hele the palsye and many other ewyls

Agnus Castus, 14th century

Bruises   Lavender is a remarkable remedy for bruises. Add a little lavender oil to witch hazel and steep a cotton compress for a few moments before applying to the injured area. This compress may also be used to reduce swelling or bruises about the eye.

Burns Dr Jean Valnet used lavender oil to treat serious burns and war injuries when he was a French army surgeon. A small burn will immediately feel better with a drop or two of lavender oil. Even a second degree burn has been known to heal within a week when treated with repeated applications of lavender oil.

Cold Feel as though you're coming down with a cold? An old folk remedy from Dorset advises that two drops of lavender essence under the nostrils will keep it at bay. Try either a full bath or a hot foot bath to induce perspiration and eliminate the toxins causing the cold. Add lavender and eucalyptus oils to the water.

Colic The distilled water of lavender, like dill water, was a familiar medicine for nurses to give their charges when they were troubled with 'the frets', the old name for 'wind'. Try a very small amount of lavender oil in the bath water to help your miserable infant to sleep. Dilute the oil first in a little almond oil and a teaspoon of vodka, otherwise the lavender oil will float in a film on the water's surface.

Cough A few drops of lavender oil may be massaged into the throat to ease a ticklish cough. The herb's sedative action will calm the irritation and dryness while the warmth of the body will release some of the volatile oil to be breathed in, thus working on the cause of the cough—the infection in the respiratory tract.

Cystitis Topical application of lavender oil is a boon for those women who are at the mercy of cystitis or thrush. Drinking plenty of lavender tea will also help cleanse the system.

Depression Due to its 'balancing' effect, lavender is very useful for treating people who are emotionally upset, or suffering from hysteria or depression. Massage on either side of the spine will help, as will lavender baths at night.

A Sweet Scented Bath

Take of Roses, Citron Peel, Orange Flowers, Lavender, Jessamy, Bays, Rosemary, Mint, Pennyroyal, of each a sufficient quantity, boil them together gently and make a Bath to which add Oyl of Spike six drops, musk five grains, Ambergris three grains.

Five Hundred Receipts, by John Middleton, 1734

Detoxification Lavender's antiseptic properties make it an important herb for cleansing the system. Drinking several cups of lavender tea every day will help flush harmful toxins from the body. In particular, try this if you work in or live near a polluted area.

Disinfectant Lavender oil is a very effective disinfectant. Roman soldiers were issued with lavender tincture which they rubbed into their wounds so the antiseptic qualities could aid healing. It was used for swabbing wounds in World Wars I and II, and was much in demand in field hospitals and emergency aid stations, where it was used to wipe down floors and bench surfaces in operating theatres. French nurses would hang cotton wool doused in lavender oil by the flaps of tents where injured soldiers lay, to repel flies.

Earache Lavender is of great relief when treating earache. Put one drop of lavender in warm water, wet a cloth with it and hold over the sore spot. Or soak a cotton wool ball in lavender oil and very gently pack the outer ear with it. The healing vapours find their way into the inner ear, and take away the pain.

Eczema Combined with chamomile, or used alone, lavender may be added to bathwater to soothe inflamed or irritated skin. This is also an excellent treatment for a child suffering from chicken pox or heat rash.

Eyes Sore, bloodshot eyes? Lavender compresses will help ease irritation and have an anti-inflammatory effect on the eyes. Bathing eyes with cooled lavender tea will also relieve strain.

And first the lavender hath the vertue of heating and drying . . . And now, if any applieth the Lavender often to the nose, in smelling thereto, it doth comforte and cleare the sighte.

The Proffitable Arte of Gardeninge, by Thomas Hyll, 1568

Fever Soothe a feverish child by offering as many glasses of cool, sweetened lavender water as he will take. It will not further irritate the inflamed throat or upset stomach which may be causing his temperature, and will help bring the fever down.

The distilled water of Lavender smelt unto, of the temples and forehead bathed therewith, is as refreshing to them that have the Catalepsie, a light migram, and to them that have the falling sickness and that use to swoune much . . . Made into powder and given to drinke in the distilled water thereof doth helpe the parting and passion of the harte, prevaileth against giddiness, turning or swimming of the braine.

The New Herball, by John Gerard, 1597

Flu   Aromatherapists claim bathing regularly with oil of lavender will help build up resistance to flu and other respiratory infections by increasing the body's production of health cells. When lavender oil is used in the treatment of cold or flu as a bath or stimulating rub, it has the ability to encourage the growth of white blood cells so the invading viruses are destroyed more quickly.

Giddiness   If you feel debilitated on a very hot day, do as the wasp-waisted maidens of the Victorian era did—reach for lavender smelling salts to ward off 'the vapours'.

Headaches   Even a spray of lavender worn beneath a hat will keep a headache at bay, as lavender farmers of old well knew. It was apparently a notable fact that they never suffered from headaches, despite working in the bright sunshine for many hours. If you feel a bad headache coming on, drink some lavender tea to help clear the head and alleviate any tummy upset which may be causing the headache. Then, gently apply lavender oil to pulse points on the forehead, and lie down for ten minutes.

Hiccups   A few well-chewed lavender leaves will often stop hiccups.

Insect Bites   Country folk once recommended the following treatment for a bite from a scorpion or spider: steep lavender heads in cold water and apply as a poultice to the inflammation till the poultice becomes warm. Then bury the lavender in a muddy bog, and the venom will travel with it! Though I suggest any scorpion or spider bite be promptly attended to by a doctor, you might like to try applying an infusion of lavender flowers on a compress to reduce swelling and redness of antbites. Crushed lavender leaves are soothing when rubbed on a bee sting and will stop the irritation spreading and infection entering.

Insomnia   In Paris the story is told of an actress, famous towards the end of the last century, who had a bunch of lavender sent to her every day for thirty years by an admirer. Each night at bedtime she would strip off the flowers and make an infusion from them to help her sleep.

It is not by accident that lavender has found its way into the herbal 'sleep pillows' so beloved by cottage craft shops. Even people picking a bunch of flowers or stripping them from their stalks for harvesting have been observed to yawn widely as they do so. Lavender oil acts as a natural sedative, toning and calming the nerves with no 'hung-over' effects. It helps to relax the nervous system, soothing knotted muscles and encouraging you to sleep relaxed and wake refreshed, even after a short nap. A few drops of the oil on a handkerchief or pillowcase can be very effective, and one or two drops on pyjamas will comfort a child frightened by nightmares.

Massage Lavender oil may be massaged onto bruises and sprains, or rubbed into chillblains. It may also be blended with another oil, such as bergamot, marjoram or rosemary, and used as a warming body rub.

Meditation Lavender oil is much used by therapists who recommend meditation techniques because it creates a harmonious atmosphere wherein mind and body can strive for balance. Psychics who practice past life therapy also favour wearing lavender essence, claiming it creates a tranquil mood, helps them focus spiritual concentration and memory, and absorbs negative attitudes.

Muscle Cramps Rub a generous amount of lavender tincture into the area of muscle cramp or spasm. If the cramps are induced by exercise, try taking long sedative baths after the jog or tennis match, adding 500ml of lavender vinegar to the bath water.

Nausea The bruised aromatic leaves of lavender act as a powerful tonic and help allay nausea. Add a little powdered lavender to a cup of hot peppermint tea to freshen the mouth and soothe the stomach.

This is called Lavender. If this be sodden in water give that water to drink to a man that hath the palsy and it will heal him. It is hot and dry.

Here begynnyth a new matter the whiche sheweth and treateth of ye vertues and propyrtes of herbes the whiche is called an Herball Imprinted by me Richard Banckes, etc, 1525

Nervous Tension Elizabeth I sipped lavender tisanes to cure her frequent tension headaches, and would dab her fretful brow with scented lavender water. Lavender oil is a soothing nervine, or nerve tonic. Massage it into the temples and back of the neck, then knead it into the hair line to ease tension quickly. It is also a good idea to brush your hair thoroughly from underneath, thus drawing out tension you have accumulated in your scalp.

Overindulgence An old wives' tale tells us that a bunch of lavender flowers worn at the neck or on a lapel helps to prevent drunkenness. Counteract post-party fatigue and alcoholic fumes by drinking plenty of lavender tea.

Palpitations The action of lavender on the muscle of the heart is sedative, making it very useful in treating palpitations and in reducing high blood pressure. Older people, who often experience uncomfortable 'hot flushes' may benefit from massage, or tepid aromatic baths containing lavender oil.

Panic In circumstances of panic or shock, and for the feeling of faintness experienced with sunstroke, simply hold a bottle of lavender essence under the nose and rub a few drops into the back of the neck. Lavender is useful in an emergency because it works quickly and restores the patient's equilibrium in a matter of moments.

Psoriasis If you suffer from psoriasis, tinea or athlete's foot, bathing with lavender and honey has an antiseptic, purifying effect. A few drops of lavender may also be massaged into the affected area. To prepare your bath, melt ½ cup of raw honey in an infusion of lavender flowers and add to water.

For gout that is cold . . . take cowslip sage, lavender, red nettle and primrose and seethe them in water and wash the place with water and it shall be helped.

A Leech Book, or, Collection of Recipes of the Fifteenth Century, by W.R. Dawson, 1934

Rheumatism Lavender oil will warm and relieve the pain of stiff joints, so it is marvellous for those suffering from rheumatism, arthritis or sciatica. Medical staff in repatriation hospitals have used lavender oil in massage treatments to exercise paralysed limbs—this was known as 'Oleum Spicae'. Rheumatic sufferers should also take

Stoechas . . . is an herb with slender twiggs, having yet haire like Thyme, but yet longer leaved and sharp in ye taste . . . but ye decoction of it is good for ye griefs in ye thorax. It is also mingled profitably with Antidots.

Dioscorides, c. 60AD

regular lavender baths, and drink lavender tea to help cleanse the system.

Sinusitis   Add a teaspoon of powdered, dried lavender flowers to water, and take it five times a day. This helps those suffering from allergic attacks of sinusitis, especially the congestion brought on by hay fever.

Skin Problems   Lavender is both antiseptic and analgesic which makes it an ideal choice for treating all kinds of skin disorders. It also promotes rapid healing and helps to prevent scarring. The oil may be used in the treatment of dermatitis, sores, varicose veins, scalds and other wounds. Whether the oil is neat or diluted in water, it has the unique ability to reduce heat, minimise pain and, at the same time, calm the patient. Blend a little oil of lavender into your favourite cream to soften chapped hands; add it to bathwater to heal skin lesions or minor burns.

Sunburn   Lavender is an essential item in the holiday suitcase. Use the oil for sunburnt noses and shoulders. For very bad sunburn, dilute the oil in a mist atomiser and gently spray the whole body to cool and soothe the injured skin.

Travel sickness   The effect of lavender oil on the brain and nervous system is very pronounced. For travel sickness, or vertigo, put a few drops of lavender oil on a sugar lump and take twice a day. Lavender is also marvellous for helping a jaded body adjust to jet lag. On arriving at your destination, run a warm bath, and pour in a generous amount of ylang-ylang and lavender. This blend is very relaxing, and will soothe you to sleep.

Lavender is . . . good to gargle the mouth with the decoction of the flowers against the paines of the teeth. Two spoonsful of the distilled water of the flowers taken, doth help those that have lost theyre speech or voyce, restoring it them again.

Theatrum Botanicum, by John Parkinson, 1640

Tiredness   In 1746 the London Pharmacopeia claimed that "... a tea brewed from Lavender Toppes, made in moderate strength, is excellent to relieve fatigue and exhaustion, giving the same relief as the application of Lavender Water to the Temples." These remedies continue to hold true today—take a strong tisane of lavender if you are in need of a pick-me-up.

... it is good also against the bitings of serpents, mad-dogs and other venomous creatures, being given inwardly and applied poultice-wise to the parts wounded.

The English Herbal, by William Salmon, 1710

Ulcers   Mouth ulcers are often a side effect of illness, or a sign of being generally run-down. A decoction of lavender flowers mixed with honey will help heal such ulcers and fight any infection in the mouth. Take three drops of lavender essence in a glass of water and hold in the mouth, rinsing slowly before spitting it out.

Vapour Inhalation   For a potent inhalant mixture, add a handful of dried lavender flowers to boiling water, along with three drops of lavender essence to intensify fragrance. Place head over a basin containing this steaming liquid and cover with a towel. This is an effective anti-viral treatment and will help deal with coughs, colds and bronchitis. Use a steam inhalation to soothe a sore throat, counter bacteria and relieve congestion.

Whooping Cough   Whooping cough and croup are two respiratory diseases which can be quite frightening, both for the child and the parent. Lavender's antispasmodic properties will have a calming effect. Try a hot compress on the patient's chest to facilitate breathing and massage a few drops of lavender oil on either side of the nose. The latter stimulates some acupressure points which help relieve congestion.

Oh, and if you are visiting a friend who is ill, you may be interested to learn that a posy of lavender is welcome as a 'get well' gift. The blue flowers were thought quite lucky, as opposed to ill-omened white or red flowers.

Lavender about the House

Traditionally, lavender was used as a strewing herb for floors and cupboards in an attempt to keep the amosphere sweet and clean in days when houses lacked protection from the damp.

The dried flowers were placed in beds and oaken presses where they perfumed handkerchiefs and linen, causing Izaak Walton to sigh longingly in 1653: "Let's go into that house, for the linen looks white and smells of lavender, and I long to be in a pair of sheets that smell so". During Elizabethan times, it was usual to sprinkle lavender water on the floors of houses, and lavender seeds would be pounded in a mortar and the aromatic oil rubbed into oak furniture to give a high gloss.

Apart from enjoying the cheerful, homely scent, housekeepers knew that lavender was a powerful weapon against the attacks of moths, silverfish and other insects. Lavender oil was dabbed around window sills to repel mosquitoes and ants, and the flowers were sewn into curtain hems to shoo away flies.

In those bygone days, the still room was the heart of every home. Here the lady of the house would distil and

... tyed up with small bundles of lavender toppes; these they put in the middle of them to lye upon the toppes of beds, presses, etc. ... from the sweet scent and savour it casteth

Paradisi in Sole Paradisus Terrestris, by John Parkinson, Apothecary of London, 1629

And still she slept,
an azure-lidded sleep,
In blanched linen,
smooth and lavender'd

The Eve of St Agnes, by
John Keats, 1818

dry her fresh lavender. She would then prepare it in a number of decorative ways, with the same aim in mind—keeping the atmosphere fresh and fragrant. Potpourri, scented candles, fragrant beads, small 'swete bags' for hanging in cupboards, sachets for laying in drawers, on shelves and in linen presses, cushions and pillows for beds and chairs all became usual accessories in every home. Special items for display in a formal parlour would be decorated with fine embroidery.

Much as the quiet pursuits of the still room worked their magic in days of yore, so will living in a lavender-scented home help to calm, comfort and uplift you. Share your enjoyment of this lovely and useful plant by preparing simple gifts for friends which are as much fun to give as to receive.

Lavender and the Daily Round

φ Lavender oil will help deter fleas from your home. Mix 1 tbspn of the oil with 1 litre of warm water, pour into pump atomiser and spray a fine mist over carpets.

φ Take your cue from one of Edna Walling's clients, who asked her to plant French lavender by her laundry door for the express purpose of drying her handkerchiefs there. Plant a lavender hedge by the clothes line and drape shirts and pillow cases there to freshen them.

φ A delightful French custom, derived from the medieval use of 'casting bottles' of perfume: instead of sprinkling water onto ironing, fill an atomiser with lavender water and use this when steaming out stubborn wrinkles.

And if any boyleth the Lavender in water and that a shyrtte wette in the same, and after dried againe (be worne) wyll suffer no Louse after to abyde in that shyrtte, so long as the shyrtte keapeth the smell.

The Profittable Arte of Gardeninge, by
Thomas Hylle, 1568

φ When washing delicate woollens or silk, remember the sentimental tale of "Sweet Lavender" penned by Sir Arthur Pinero in 1888. In this play, the heroine is a humble laundress who used lavender water to scent freshly-washed clothes . . . including those of the King, who sought her out and asked for her hand in marriage, so impressed was he! Even if you are not seeking a royal betrothal, try adding a few drops of lavender essence to the final rinse water. It will remove any traces of suds and fill the clothes with fragrance, as well as acting as a moth repellent.

φ Remember how Grandma's furniture used to gleam and shine? By adding lavender oil to your dusting rag, you can have a similar sheen on your precious woodwork.

φ Flies will steer clear of your home if it is filled with the wholesome scent of lavender. Add a few drops to a jug of water and place it in the corner of a room.

φ Ants heartily dislike lavender, too—a few drops by their nest will soon send them scurrying. By the same token, plant lavender bushes by an aviary or henhouse, if you have one, as this will stop bird lice from annoying your pets.

φ Arrange dried lavender flowers and leaves in a pretty container—look for a wicker basket, old copper kettle, earthenware pot or pewter mug. Or hang bunches from the rafter or by your mantelpiece, where the warmth of a fire will strengthen the fragrance. Sprinkle a few drops of lavender oil on the arrangement if the scent starts to fade.

φ Place a drop of lavender oil on a light bulb. When it is switched on and becomes warm, the scent will fill the whole room.

φ Enjoying a roaring log fire in the evening? Make it a "scentual" experience by throwing a handful of lavender potpourri on the flames to freshen the room. A charming housewarming gift would be bunches of dried lavender and rosemary twigs, bundled together and labelled for this purpose.

φ Lavender finger bowls will set a stylish note at your next dinner party. Tie up tiny posies of lavender and lemon-scented verbena with florists' wire and drop them in guests' finger bowls.

Velvet gown and dainty fur
Should be laid in lavender
For its sweetness drives away
Fretting moths of silver-grey

A Bunch of Sweet Lavender, by
Constance Isherwood, c. 1900

Sweet Sleep Pillow

Lavender scented candles freshen the room

φ Christmas? Easter? Birthday or family celebration? The Victorians dearly loved lavender and, being sentimentalists, would weave garlands of lavender, rosemary and evergreen to be hung about the portrait of the family founder on such important occasions.

A Celebration of Lavender

The popularity of sachets, potpourri and other fragrant household items is evidence of a realisation that our surroundings, as well as ourselves, can be made more pleasant by being scented. As Abraham Crowley succinctly noted in the 17th century:-

"Who that hath reason, and his smell
Wouldst not among roses and Jasmine dwell?
Rather than all his spirits choke
With exhalations of dirt and smoke?"

POTPOURRI

This well-known term refers to scented leaves and flowers, combined with a fixative, which are enjoyed for their long-lasting fragrance. There are two popular methods—dry potpourri and moist potpourri. Lavender's sweet, camphoraceous scent lends itself best to the dry potpourri method. Keep an eye out for antique lidded sugar bowls, pretty serving dishes, silver trays or unusual jars to display your lavender potpourri in.

Harvest lavender flowers and leaves mid-morning, after dew has dried. Place on racks lined with paper and dry in a slow oven. Combine lavender in a bowl with other ingredients, then mix in oils and orris root powder. You might like to add a few drops of brandy to strengthen the scent. Place the mixture in a dark, airtight container and store for a month to mature, shaking the contents regularly. Try any of the following recipes:-

No bought potpourri is so pleasant as that made from one's own garden, for the petals of the flowers . . . hold the sunshine and memories of summer, and . . . only the sunny days should be remembered.

The Scented Garden, by Eleanour Sinclair Rohde

NURSERY POTPOURRI

A soft, refreshing perfume for Baby's room.

250g lavender flowers
125g rose petals
125g lemon verbena
50g marjoram
1 tbspn dried lemon rind
2 tbspn orris root
essential oils—rose and lavender

APHRODISIAC POTPOURRI

A warm and dusky mood-setter.

250g lavender flowers
125g jasmine flowers
125g orange flowers
1 tbspn sandalwood powder
2 tbspn orris root powder
essential oils—musk and lavender

KITCHEN SUNSHINE POTPOURRI

Tangy and energising in the kitchen, this helps keep flies
away—and it's pretty to look at, too!

250g lavender flowers
25g marigold flowers
25g yellow everlasting daisies
100g lemon thyme
100g lemon balm
cinnamon powder
bay leaves
2 tbspn orris root powder
essential oils—lemon and lavender

POTPOURRI IN THE SICK ROOM

Cleansing and refreshing for a patient with cold or flu.

250g lavender flowers
100g lemon thyme
100g peppermint
2 tbspn lemon rind
2 tsp nutmeg chips
essential oils—lavender and peppermint

MY FAVOURITE BLEND

Pretty and relaxing, try this In the guests' bedroom or
welcoming them at the front door.

150g lavender
150g pink rose petals
50g chamomile daisies
50g carnation flowers
1 crushed vanilla pod
2 tsp cloves
2 tbspn orris root powder
essential oils—lavender and carnation

SACHETS AND 'SWETE BAGS'

Pretty sachets have a place in every home. Hang them
wherever they may be brushed against or where passers-
by will occasionally squeeze them to release the scent. Use
a variety of fabrics to make your sachets—gingham, sprigged
muslin and embroidered lawn are suitable—and experiment
with shapes and sizes. How about a lacy, heart-shaped 'swete
bag' for Valentine's Day? Or a soft bolster for a new mother
to lean against whilst feeding her baby? The possibilities
are only limited by your imagination . . .

. . . on the backs of my armchairs are thin Liberty silk oblong bags, like miniature saddle bags, filled with dried lavender . . . the visitor who leans back in his chair wonders from where the scent comes.

Potpourri from a Surrey Garden, by Mrs Earle, 1900

φ Stitch pretty little purses of mauve voile and fill with lavender. Trim with fine lace or a bow of purple and green ribbons. Hang on hooks at the back of your wardrobe.

φ Different lavender potpourri mixes may be used in sachets and 'swete bags' in different parts of the house:-

In the kitchen, make small calico bags and fill them with lavender, lemon verbena and cloves.

For the lingerie drawer, I like lavender flowers with rose-scented geranium leaves. To increase the perfume, add two drops of lavender essence.

Freshen the bathroom by tucking sachets containing lavender and lemon-scented tea-tree amongst towels.

For the menfolk, fill that wardrobe of suits with a breath of fresh air . . . lavender, lemon verbena and mint smell clean and invigorating.

φ The best moth-deterrent of all is a combination of crushed bay leaves, camphor and lavender. Either pack into sachets and fold amongst linen, or scatter powdered mix over shelves and in boxes.

POMANDERS

This word is derived from the French 'pomade', meaning 'apple-shaped'. It is attributed to Henry V who was never without a 'ball of gold' packed with musk grains and lavender seeds that he acquired during his victory at Agincourt. Elizabeth I wore 'a fayre gyrdle of small pomenders strung like a necklace' about her hips. Made of gold and silver filigree, each contained a different scent.

Hanged up in houses in the heate of sommer, doth very well attemper the aire, coole and make fresh the place, to the delight and comfort of such as are therein.

The Herball, by John Gerard, 1597

Like sachets and potpourri, pomanders have a long history of use—as ornamentation, to cure insomnia, as perfumes and as antiseptic agents during times of illness. Hang these pretty, sweet-smelling fruits in your linen press; place a selection of them in a wicker basket near a window, or fold them amongst handkerchiefs in your drawers.

LAVENDER-LIME POMANDER

I large lime
25 cloves
I tbspn orris root powder
I tbspn powdered lavender flowers

Insert clove heads all over skin of fruit, leaving space where ribbon will be bound. Dust lime with orris root and lavender powders, wrap in tissue and leave to dry for three weeks.

For decoration, glue dried lavender flowers and leaves to mauve satin ribbon tied about pomander.

INCENSE

The first man-made perfumes were a by-product of fire, lavender being one of the sacred aromatic plants early man burnt to attract good spirits, dispel evil and encourge prophetic dreams.

Lavender was once an ingredient in incense used for religious and spiritual rituals. It was much favoured by the French Catholic Church, and nuns burnt lavender pastilles stamped with their convent's insignia during Masses. Montaigne wrote of the scent that ". . . in churches . . . (it) . . . had an especial regard to rejoyce, to comforte, to quicken and to rouse, and to purifie our sense."

Lavender incense is particularly appropriate in a musty sick room, where its aroma is much appreciated by the convalescent. A very simple method is to sprinkle a few drops of lavender oil on a heated metal dish—or, try one of the following recipes:-

LAVENDER INCENSE STICKS

Remove the flower heads from a handful of long stems of lavender and soak in saltpetre. Allow to dry thoroughly. Place dried stalks in terracotta jar or enamel pot and light as you would a stick of incense.

LAVENDER INCENSE PASTILLES

1 tsp lavender oil
100g gum benzoin
3 tsp gum tragacanth
200g charcoal
30g cascarilla bark

Grind dry ingredients together, then add resins and oil. Blend thoroughly, adding a little cold water if needed. Mould pastilles, about 1" diameter.
Note: Charcoal will make the pastilles burn well enough to release the aroma of lavender; however, a little saltpetre may be added to keep them burning longer.

LAVENDER SCENTED CANDLES

A candle packed with fresh lavender or a tall mauve one decorated with a sprig of the flowers will freshen a room and induce sweet dreams. They also make a charming gift.

Wax, wicks, colouring and moulds are readily available at craft shops. Melt the wax, add the hardener which the manufacturer recommends, and insert the wick into the mould. Add dried lavender stalks, snipped to short lengths with scissors, and a few drops of lavender essence to the wax just before pouring it into the mould.

Decorate your candle by pressing lavender flowers into a pattern round it. "Iron" the flowers into place by smoothing the wax gently with a warm dry spoon. Then paint over with a little clear paraffin, to create a transparent glaze.

. . . and lavender, whose spikes of azure bloom
shall be erewhile, in arid bundles bound,
To lurk amidst the labours of her loom,
And crown her kerchiefs clean with mickle rare perfume.

The Schoolmistress, by William Shenstone, 1742

A GIFT OF LAVENDER

A lavender bush itself makes a lovely present. Make it all the more memorable by potting it in a terracotta tub, and then stencil the rim with a pattern of mauve flowers and dots, and green leaves. Or gift-wrap the base in purple tissue or tulle.

A delightful Chinese custom involves small children tying paper flowers and 'wishes' to the branches of lucky trees. Adapt this idea by writing messages such as "Happy Birthday" on a dozen strips of purple paper and then twist them round the branches of a chosen tree or shrub.

Simple gifts can be made very special if lavender is used in their preparation. The following ideas embody just what gift-giving should be—personal, created with the recipient's tastes foremost in mind, and as much fun to make as to give!

Lavender Fan

Once upon a time ladies' fans commanded an entire language privy only to lovers. Have a romantic flutter on a hot day by decorating your straw fan with a bunch of dried lavender and a sachet of potpourri tied on with mauve velvet ribbon. The scent is very refreshing as the fan sways to and fro.

Lavender Toys

Children love old-fashioned, lavender-scented rag dolls, and toys for puppies and kittens which are stuffed with lavender help keep fleas away, as well as being playthings.

Either purchase a pattern for a soft toy from your craft shop, or draft simple shapes, such as teddies, rabbits or fish onto two pieces of material. Remember to leave a seam allowance all the way around. Embroider a face and other details on the front and add dried flowers to wadding before sewing up the toy.

For ambitious seamstresses, a doll with an elegant wardrobe may be in order for a small girl. Miss Lavender Dolly could sport a mauve pinny delicately perfumed with lavender, along with a lavender-decked bonnet and bag— even her own lavender cushion to sit upon.

Lavender is almost wholly spent with us for to perfume linnen, apparell, gloves and leather and the dryed flowers to comfort and dry up the moisture . . .

Theatrum Botanicum, by John Parkinson, 1640

Oven Mitts

Lavender-scented oven mitts are very easy to make. Simply unpick a seam and tuck dried lavender into the padding where your palm will go. Then, sew it up. A refreshing burst of fragrance will be released each time the mitt is squeezed round a hot dish.

The smell . . . hidden in the green
Pour'd back into my empty soul
and frame
The times when I remembered to
have been
Joyful and free from blame

Alfred, Lord Tennyson

Lavender Drawer Liners

Take lengths of thick parchment-style paper—floral wallpaper is ideal—and cut to fit the inside of your drawer. Cover with dried lavender or lavender potpourri, roll up lengths and seal in plastic bags. After six weeks the paper will have absorbed the perfume. To intensify fragrance, dab a few drops of lavender oil on a cotton ball and wipe round the inside of each drawer before placing paper inside.

Sweet Sleep Pillow

His Majesty George III was said to rely upon a lavender-scented pillow to ". . . relieve him from that protracted wakefulness under which he laboured for so long a time".

To make a lavender sleep pillow, stitch two squares of fabric together on three sides. The lavender, along with other ingredients, may be mixed with the pillow stuffing or put into sachet bags and placed inside the pillows. For the hedonist who wants to snuggle down into balmy dreams of summer, try the following combination to lull you to sleep:-

> *"Lavender Dream"*
> 25g lavender flowers
> 25g rosemary leaves
> 15g rose geranium leaves
> 25g jasmine petals
> handful crushed cloves
> 1 tbspn orris root

Lavender Wand

A favourite lavender gift is the scented 'bottle', or wand. Pick abour 30 lavender flowers on stalks as long as possible. With a narrow ribbon about a metre long, tie the heads tightly together just below the flowers. Bend the stems back gently below the ribbon so they form a cage over the flowers, and tie the stems together. Weave the long end of ribbon over and under the stems, moving down till all the lavender is enclosed. Stitch the ribbon ends securely, and finish with a bow.

Scented Coathangers

Lavender is the scent that immediately springs to mind for hanging with clothes. Fill a muslin bag the length of your coathanger with lavender or lavender sachet mix. Then sew it in place on top of the hanger, before covering with pretty silk, organza or muslin. A finishing touch—swing a tiny 'swete bag' of lace-trimmed matching fabric from the hook.

Lavender Notepaper

Store sheets of paper and envelopes, preferably tinted soft pink or mauve, in a box, liberally sprinkling each layer with lavender. An olde-worlde crinkled effect may be given to the paper by misting with a spray of lavender water before drying.

Decorate your notepaper by mounting a few dried lavender flowers onto each sheet with transparent craft glue. If it is to be a gift, a charming accessory is scented ink— add 1 tspn of lavender essence to a bottle of purple ink for truly deathless prose!

Lavender Scented Beads

In the court of Elizabeth I, louche ladies-in-waiting wore bracelets made of small wax beads perfumed with lavender, which were believed effective against the dreaded 'pox'. Latterly, Victorian girls threaded such beads into necklaces and exchanged them as party favours. Try making a pretty piece of scented jewellery for yourself or for a friend; the fragrance intensifies with the warmth of the skin and will last many years.

> 4 tbspn lavender powder
> 4 tbspn gum tragacanth
> 4 tbspn orris root
> lavender oil
> hat pin and fishing line

Blend all dry ingredients, add gum and mix to a paste. Dip your hands in oil, pick up pinches of the mix and roll in your palms to form beads. Place on waxed paper and leave overnight. Take hat pin and dip in oil. Pierce each bead and hang on line. Wrap in tissue and store in dark place for 6 weeks.

Lavender, lavender
That makes your linen sweet;
The hawker brings his basket
Down the sooty street.

Alfred Noyes

On the shelves used to be bundles of sweet marjoram and pennyroyal and lavender and mint and catnip . . . the odourous echoes of a score of dead summers linger yet in those dim recesses . . .

A Song of Other Days, by
Oliver Wendell Holmes, 1858

Headache Pillow

Lavender helps clear the head and induce sleep. Fill a soft pillow with dried lavender, lime blossoms and scented geranium leaves. Give to a fractious patient suffering from headache, earache or fever.

Travel Pillow

Many people become apprehensive when travelling, whether through fear or actual motion sickness. A gift much appreciated by queasy travellers is a soft neck-cushion— kidney-shaped is best, as it will support the head—filled with lavender and mint to soothe jangled nerves.

Lavender Pin Cushion

Make sewing even more enjoyable by slipping a lavender sachet into your pincushion. Every time you press a pin or needle home, a puff of scent will be released, perfuming both the work and the seamstress.

Scented Pajama Case

When making a case for storing your night attire, fill the space between the lining and the outer case with lavender. This will perfume your sheets and enfold you in a delicate cloud of scent all night long. Choose pretty cotton or silk to match the bed linen, and edge the case with ribbon.

Padded Drawer Liners

These are made by cutting fine organdy or taffeta rectangular pouches to fit the base of your drawers. Stitch on three sides, fill sparingly with a fragrant mixture of lavender potpourri, then stitch the fourth seam. Placed in each drawer, these padded drawer liners will effectively perfume your clothes as well as the room.

——————— AN ODD SPOT . . . ———————

The Rev Dion Clayton Calthorp so loved the fragrance of his lavender bush that he penned this fanciful tribute for a tombstone marker when it was pruned:-

Here Lies
Imprisoned in this grey bush
the scent of
LAVENDER
It is renowned for a Simple Purity
A Sweet Fragrance and a Subtle Strength
It is the odour of Domestic Virtues and
The symbolic perfume of a Quiet Life
Rain
shall weep over This Bush
Sun
shall give it Sweet Kisses
Wind
shall stir the tall spikes
until such a time as is required
when it shall Flower
and so
yield to us its Secret

Bibliography

The Gardener's Folklore
  M. Baker
  David & Charles, London, 1977

Herbs for Health and Beauty
  S. Beedel
  Sphere, London, 1972

Old Wives' Lore for Gardeners
  M. and B. Boland
  The Bodley Head, 1976

The Illustrated Flower
  S. Chwast and B. Chewning
  Australia & New Zealand Book Co., 1977

Liqueurs for all Seasons
  E. Cocconi
  Lyceum Books, USA, 1975

The Lore and Legends of Flowers
  R. L. Crowell
  Crowell, NY, 1982

The Complete Herbal
  N. Culpeper
  Manchester, 1826

Culpeper's Herbal Remedies
  N. Culpeper
  Wilshire Book Co., Ca., 1971

Aromatherapy—an A-Z
  P. Davis
  C. W. Daniel, England, 1988

Natural Skin Care
  C. de Haas
  Nature & Health Books, 1986

Herbal Medicine
  D. Dincin Buchman
  Hutchinson Group Ltd., Great Britain, 1983

The Healing Power
  N. Drury
  Australia & New Zealand Book Co., 1981

Healing Oils & Essences
  N. and S. Drury
  Harper & Row, 1987

A Book of Potpourri
  G. Duff
  Orbis Publishing, 1985

Presents from Your Garden
  N. Dutton
  Nelson Australia, 1986

The Herbal Medicine Chest
  N. Evelyn
  Second Back Row Press, 1983

The Story of Lavender
  S. Festing
  Heritage in Sutton Leisure, 1989

The Origins of Garden Plants
  J. Fisher
  Constable London, 1960

Proverbs & Sayings of Ireland
  ed: S. Gaffney and S. Cashman
  The Wolfhound Press, Dublin, 1974

A Gardener's Potpourri
  ed: T. R. Garnett
  Nelson, Australia, 1986

A Book of Aromatics
  R. Genders
  Darton Longman & Todd, London, 1978

The Herbal
  J. Gerard
  Dover Publications Inc., NY, 1975

Green Magic
  L. Gordon
  Webb & Bower, London/Ebury Press,
  1977

Aromatherapy: Australian Text book
  B. Greenwood
  Cleopatra's Needle, 1989

Potpourri & Perfumery from Australian
  Gardens
  D. Greig
  Kangaroo Press, 1986

A Modern Herbal
  Mrs M. Grieve
  Penguin, 1984

The Womens' Book of Natural Beauty
  A. Guyton
  Thorsons Publishers Ltd., 1984

The Origin of Rhymes, Songs and Sayings
  J. Harrowven
  Kaye and Ward, 1977

Herbs & Spices
  J. & R. Hemphill
  Summit Books: Paul Hamlyn, 1978

Herbs for Health
  J. & R. Hemphill
  Landsowne Press, Australia, 1986

Fragrance & Flavour
  R. Hemphill
  Angus & Robertson, 1972

Plants for Natural Beauty Care
  B. Hlaug, F. Popsil, F. Stary
  Cathay Books, GB, 1981

Natural Beauty
  L. Horrocks
  Angus & Robertson, 1983

Aromatherapy
  J. Jackson
  Greenhouse Publications, Victoria, 1987

Old Time Herbs for Northern Gardens
  M. W. Kamm
  Dover Publications, London, 1974

The Book of the Bath
  C. Kanner
  Piatkus Books, London, 1986

The Faithful Garden
  F. Kelly
  Methuen, Australia, 1986

A Perfumed Garden
  F. Kelly
  Methuen, Australia, 1981

The Gentle Art of Flavouring
  R. Landry
  Abelard: Schuman, NY, 1972

Herbs—How to Grow and Use Them
  M. Leth
  Harrap, London, 1986

Herbal Delights
  Mrs C. F. Leyel
  Faber & Faber, 1987

The Complete Book of Herbs & Spices
  C. Loewenfeld and P. Beck
  A. H. & A. W. Reed, Wellington, NZ,
  1974

Garden Herbs for Australia and New
  Zealand
  C. MacDonald
  A. H. & A. W. Reed, Sydney, 1978

The Book of Lavender
  J. A. McLeod
  Wild Woodbine Studio, 1982

Sachets, Potpourri and Incense
  D. C. Meyer
  Meyerbooks, USA, 1986
The World of Herbs
  J. Mitchel & L. Lynch
  Macmillan Australia, 1985
The Oxford Dictionary of Nursery Rhymes
  I. & P. Opie
  The Clarendon Press, 1975
Paradisi in Sole Paradisus Terrestris
  J. Parkinson
  London, 1629
Flowers of the World
  F. Perry
  Hamlyn, New York, 1972
The Meaning of Flowers
  C. Powell
  Jupiter Books, London, 1977
From Me to You
  E. Renshaw and S. King
  Collins Sydney, Australia, 1984
A Garden of Herbs
  E. S. Rohde
  Dover Publications Inc., NY, 1969
Kitchen Cosmetics
  J. Rose
  Panjandrum/Aris Books, 1978
The Book of Herbs
  K. N. Sanecki
  Doubleday Australia, 1985

The Mystery of Perfume
  R. Schnitzer
  Orbis, London, 1984
Encyclopaedia of Herbs and Herbalism
  M. Stuart
  Orbis, London, 1978
The Macmillan Book of Proverbs, Maxims
    and Famous Phrases
  ed: B. Stevenson
  Macmillan, NY, 1973
The Folklore of Plants
  T. F. Thistleton Dyer
  Chatto & Windus, London, 1889
Aromatherapy for Women
  M. Tisserand
  Thorsons, England, 1985
The Art of Aromatherapy
  R. Tisserand
  C. W. Daniel & Co., Ltd., UK, 1979
Herbs—How to Grow and Use Them
  S. Tomnay
  Leisure Magazines, Australia, 1988
The Romantic Story of Scent
  J. Trueman
  Aldus/Jupiter, London, 1975
Flowerworks
  H. Walden
  Simon & Schuster, 1987

Acknowledgements

The author gratefully acknowledges the assistance provided by the following people. Without their help this book would not have been possible.

Mr C. Comins, Flower Essence Services, USA

Mr P. Daffy, Blackmores Laboratories Ltd, Australia

Mr T. Denny, Bridestowe Estate, Tasmania

Mr N. Drury, Craftsman's Press, Australia

Mr H. Head, Norfolk Lavender Estate, UK

Miss R. Holmes & Miss E. Anderson, Yuulong Lavender Estate, Victoria

The resource archives of *Nature & Health Magazine*, Australia

Mr T. Rodd, Royal Botanical Gardens, Sydney

Mrs J. Stephenson, Creswick, Victoria, Australia

Mr J. Weathersbee, Yardley of London Ltd, Australia

The resource archives of *Wellbeing* magazine, Australia

Mr Ian White, Bush Flower Essences, Australia

Ms J. White & Ms K. Day, *In Essence*, Wholistic Traders Pty Ltd, Australia

The resource archives of *Your Garden* magazine, Australia